CRISIS
MANAGEMENT

What doesn't kill you, makes you stronger.

—**Nietzsche**

CRISIS MANAGEMENT

LEADERSHIP, TEAM DYNAMICS, AND RESILIENCE IN PLAY

PRACTITIONER'S PERSPECTIVE FROM COVID-19
AND OTHER Lived Experiences

Major C.T. Sadanandan

PENTAGON PRESS LLP

First published in 2023 by

PENTAGON PRESS LLP
206, Peacock Lane, Shahpur Jat
New Delhi-110049, India
Contact: 011-64706243

Typeset in Palatino, 11 Point
Printed by Aegean Offset Printers, Greater Noida, U.P.

ISBN: 978-93-90095-58-2 (HB)

www.pentagonpress.in

CONTENTS

SECTION 3
RESILIENCE IN CRISIS MANAGEMENT

Foreword

No one loves crisis yet crisis happens in every sphere of human and organizational life. Some are due to natural causes, and many are manmade when it comes to business and the economy.

Crisis management is very situational and involves dealing with chaos.

The interconnectedness of the global economy renders even small, tiny events snowball to become major catastrophes just like the butterfly effect. A crisis in its worst outcome ends in disaster.

The Chornobyl disaster is a classic example. Every crisis places enormous pressure on the system and resources, and it calls for exceptional leadership, teamwork and resilience to deal with such situations. These challenges become even more daunting when it involves the safety of people.

In this work, the author brings out the interplay of remarkable personal leadership efforts and team dynamics demonstrated during real-life experiences in crises of varying nature and magnitude.

The foremost requirement in managing any crisis is defining situational ownership and establishing a robust response and recovery mechanism. The real-life situations narrated in this book amplifies how military principles like command control system and meticulous planning are extremely important in a crisis scenario and how these were deployed in resolving the crises during IPKF military operations in Sri Lanka, flood control in Chennai or even the terror attack in Mumbai. The uniqueness is about the author's military background and how that enabled him to be disciplined while coping with the crisis and executing response strategies.

Overall, the lessons learnt from managing various crises have been brought out well and this book will serve as a playbook for managers, specifically at the operational and middle levels in business organizations called upon to respond to crises.

Dr EJ Sarma
Author, Advisor – Organization Change Management
San Jose, California, United States

Introduction

As a veteran entrepreneur leading a premium global security and risk consultancy, my job involves working with leaders of global organizations before, during, and after crises. I have known the author (I call him C. T. S.) for over a decade and have interacted with him in high-stress situations. I always admired his ability to remain calm, instil trust in the team, stay ahead of events, and emerge successfully (of course, he would only own up to the failures; the credit was always his team's).

As the world grappled with the double whammy of the pandemic—an unprecedented health crisis and a severe socioeconomic dislocation—this treatise, the author's recollection of events and experiences during the war, emergencies, and crises in various corporate leadership roles and across geographies, brings out the essence of resilience and crisis leadership.

Narrated in the form of seven first-hand gripping stories of extraordinary human accomplishments in the face of adversity, it makes for easy and compelling reading, and draws key lessons at the end of each story, every lesson based on hard-won experience and worth its weight in gold!

Emergencies and crises do not come alone. The author's candid articulation of his experiences in dealing with multi-crisis scenarios is fascinating! The importance of leading from the front, assuming responsibility, and making timely decisions in the fog of war; the need for focus and prioritizing; the importance of planning, training, and crisis communications; the battle-winning factors of trust, mutual respect, collaboration, and teamwork; crisis bringing out the best in each member, spurring them to rise to the challenge—all these make for compelling reading and learning.

The author's hard-won experience as a crisis leader, of dealing with battle and non-battle casualties during the war, and leading his teams during a range of emergencies, from natural disasters to accidents and a global crisis, and drawing out relevant lessons, makes it a most authentic comprehensive work about resilience. It is a must-read for business, government, military, community, and civil society leaders of today and tomorrow, and real-life practitioners of business continuity, resiliency, and crisis management.

I wish you happy reading!

S.M. Kumar
Co-founder and Managing Director, MitKat Advisory

Author's Note

The outbreak of the COVID-19 global pandemic in January 2020 and the rapid developments that followed posed enormous challenges and unprecedented safety risks to humanity. People were forced to accept a new way of life. The spread of a pandemic at such a rapid pace and on a global scale had never been imagined. This situation led to immense challenges for business organizations, as business continuity plans in this context did not exist. Leadership across organizations had to carefully evaluate priorities, as the critical need of the hour was to safeguard the health and safety of people while attempting to ensure the progression of business obligations to customers.

In this scenario, I along with a crack task force was entrusted with the responsibility of planning and executing a business continuity plan for a large global organization. This being an unprecedented scenario, with no playbooks to go by, leading the effort to deliver the defined outcome was a formidable task under the prevailing ambiguous and volatile environment. We were required to design, improvise, implement and enhance the response plans as we went along the unfolding and ever-changing crisis landscape.

Admirably, the team was successful in implementing a business continuity management framework to deal with this unique situation within a few weeks. While the initial response to this unprecedented situation was effective, the challenge continued in sustaining the same through a prolonged period for over two years. With frequently changing scenarios from a different manifestation of the pandemic interspersed with many other events and situations impacting business continuity and people safety, the task transformed into an enormous challenge. This was a unique situation in the history of humankind where the ability to sustain a prolonged peril was put to trial. As an organization, we were able to tide over this successfully with all the timely actions driven by the core team that worked as a cohesive unit in the face of this formidable challenge.

As the team leader, I was asked by my peers what had enabled me to achieve this rapid and successful transition from a business-as-usual operation to a business continuity management mode of operation, in such an unforeseen and daunting situation and continue to remain focused through a prolonged period of crisis. This prompted reflecting on my lived experiences to understand what are the underlying factors that enable individuals and teams to confront, manage, and live through a crisis and emerge resilient. I started penning down this in 2020 during the peak of Covid and lockdowns. The first impression was published as an e-book on Amazon Kindle in November 2020. The pandemic persisted for a prolonged period in various forms and waves and the crises and challenges that resulted from this multiplied, bringing in more learnings thus an updated version is now published as a paperback.

Through this treatise, I attempt to relate my learning on different facets of leadership principles, traits, and team dynamics that interplay in crises, through a wide array of experiences ranging from my early days as a junior leader with the Indian Army and later as a global leader in the corporate sector. This is a view from both ends of the leadership kaleidoscope—of the leader and the led from these lived experiences.

In this book, I have narrated true stories from various challenging crises that I had been part of, at different stages of my professional life. The lessons learnt from these experiences as a practising crisis manager are shared here under three distinct sections which are—crisis leadership, team dynamics in crisis and resilience in crisis.

The diverse experience gained from all the narrated incidents had a profound impact on my resilience and critical leadership skills to manage challenges. My diaries, notes, and conversations with many colleagues who were part of these crises have helped to preserve the true essence of the situations, challenges, and outcomes narrated here. Learning from each crisis is correlated to the challenges inherent in the narrated incidents. Learning has been described as relevant at the point in time of occurrence—with due care not to be influenced by my current thinking.

I am cognizant that all experiences and learning are unique. There would be many readers with numerous crises experiences—even more severe than the ones narrated herein. I believe such personal experiences need to be recorded and shared to create a powerful repository of experience-based learning that can inspire individuals and teams. I have adopted a simple language and a basic narrative style with the belief that it helps to connect the reader easily with situations. I sincerely hope this inspires all readers to reflect on their experiences under similar situations and inspires them to share their learning for a greater benefit.

SECTION 1

Leadership in Crisis Management

If you don't choose to do it in Leadership time upfront,
you do it in crisis management time down the road.

—Stephen Covey

1

The Art and Science of Crisis Leadership

One of the biggest challenges in any leadership role is managing crises that can occur in the organizations they lead. A crisis by its very nature is a situation that can have a significant adverse impact on people and organizations. These situations will be of different magnitudes and types and can occur at any time without any warning. A crisis warrants critical thinking, speedy decisions and quick actions to eliminate or minimize the risks associated with the same. Therefore, dealing with such situations calls for an entirely different style of leadership as compared to what would be under a normal or business-as-usual situation.

Academically there are various theories and different models suggested for managing a crisis. These are based on research and studies over a period and define a crisis, its characteristics and a suggested framework for adoption or implementation in a crisis. However, it will not be possible to orchestrate and practically apply these models and frameworks in their entirety in a crisis scenario, as much of it depends on the actual situation developments and resultant challenges on the ground. Therefore, the response and management of these situations would need to vary based on the unique crisis event and prevalent circumstances such as the severity of the incident, and its debilitating impact on the business processes, people and reputation of the organization. The leadership requirement would therefore be defined by the urgency, speed of response and specific actions needed to eliminate or limit the impact of the crisis. This does not imply to say that the elements of a classical model of crisis management would be irrelevant, but the leadership skill of integrating the knowledge of the theoretical frameworks with the actual response needed in a situation is the real art of managing a crisis.

In a typical crisis management framework, there are essentially four stages:

- Before the occurrence of the incident the steps involve crisis preparation wherein the probable crises and risks are identified and potential business impact from these are assessed proactively. Based on this assessment, the response mechanism, including crisis communication is defined and documented, systems and processes are put in place, and people are trained on the response process through simulations and desktop exercises. This is essentially the governance part of crisis management.

- The next step is crisis prevention which involves continuous monitoring and scanning of the environment to pick early warnings and prepare for mitigating and managing imminent risks. This involves the preparation and dissemination of documents such as emergency response plans, standard operating procedures and plans for disaster management and recovery. Rehearsal of these plans in simulated scenarios continues in this phase as well.

- Subsequent phase is managing the crisis when it occurs. This is termed crisis incident management and the process involves crisis recognition, system activation and response initiation leading to the actual management of a crisis.

- The final stage, after the crisis has occurred, is managed and is over, involves the recovery and business resumption, post-crisis impact evaluation and modification to the crisis response processes based on the learnings from the incident.

Enterprise risk management is a critical responsibility of business leaders, and it entails identifying all the possible scenarios that could harm the business and putting in place possible mitigation measures. The risk areas considered broadly would fall under market risks, technology, product and services offered by the firm, financial, workforce, political and geopolitical, natural calamities etc. Many external agencies carry out a risk assessment on an ongoing basis, typically any organization will have an internal risk management function which takes the help of these subject matter experts to prepare the risk management matrix for the organization. These plans are reviewed periodically at the apex level of the organization and the mitigation strategies are fine-tuned from time to time. However, it is not practically possible to identify and forecast which component of the assessed risk would turn out to be a crisis and at which point in time it will occur. Therefore, managing a crisis as it occurs calls for an even more different level of leadership style-especially at the operational level which would be at the forefront to lead the response to any crisis scenario.

Every manager in his/her role is expected to identify the risks within the ambit of the operations and prepare mitigation plans – like the risk management process at the organisational level. Therefore a crisis manager's role is inherent in every management position in business organizations.

Even with well-defined risk management processes existing, there would be situations that are unforeseen and unexpected for which there is no prepared response plan available for reference and action. Another situational variance would be that the operations manager or team leader who is at the forefront of the crisis, is not a part of the risk management governance and managing a crisis is not part of his/her defined role or Key Result Areas (KRA) and thus does not adequately prepare that person to deal with an unexpected emerging crisis. Most of the crises and consequent business impact can be effectively managed if these situations are reviewed, potential risks identified and quickly responded to. It is also true that even with the best of risk management and crisis response process, any risk situation if not responded to adequately at the right time can precipitate a major crisis with a debilitating impact on the organization. Therefore, preparing the first level of response is the key to effective crisis management and is the most essential skill required for a manager or leader faced with the responsibility to deal with such a situation.

The focus area for this book is crisis management and leadership at the operational level, which is the first level of response. The importance of situational leadership and the criticality of the first-level manager's ability to deal with expected and unexpected crises is highlighted through various lived experiences, narrated in this book.

The most difficult problem for a leader, when faced with a challenge, is the ability to recognize the developing situation and its potential to become a crisis. Critical thinking is the most important leadership ability required at this stage of crisis management, which requires the leader to think quickly, analyze systematically and decide speedily. Time is of the essence here – the quicker one can identify the imminent crisis, the better you are prepared to deal with it. In a rapidly changing crisis scenario, the time available will not be adequate for a deliberate process and even as defined in the guidebook to assess the risk and evaluate response options. The key leadership skill required at this juncture would be the ability to visualize potential scenarios based on the available information and assess the gravity of the emerging crisis and the potential impact based on which the response process needs to be activated and implemented.

It is possible that in the early stages of an emerging crisis, the information, or data points available or accessible are inadequate, inaccurate, conflicting, confusing or a combination of all these. The challenge therefore for the crisis manager is to sift through this fog of inadequate information. The critical leadership skill required for this would be the ability to process quick validation of the available information and data points. The best method to achieve this would be, checking through different sources, looking at the patterns and comparing them with real-time or known situations of similar nature elsewhere and accessing additional information and data points through any other available source such as other organizations or common sources like government agencies. Combined with these, a personal visit to the site of the incident would equip the leader to take decisive actions- The military adage "one look is better than one hundred reports" fits well in a crisis scenario. Being at the site in person enables the crisis leader to correlate the information or data points he has received through various sources with the situation on the ground and equips him to be in a position to make informed decisions.

The logical next step after the preliminary assessment of the emerging crisis is activating the response plan. If there are playbooks, Standard Operating Procedures (SOPs) and response processes already available, one could refer to those quickly, validate the assumptions and parameters vis-à-vis the actual ground scenario and adjust the responses. However, if the crisis is unforeseen, there would be the need to decide on what is the most important objective to be ensured while managing the crisis, put together a plan, mobilize resources and initiate the responses. The most valuable resource in these times would be the team that you are working with. It will be incumbent on the leader to garner the confidence and collaboration from various stakeholders who would need to be part of the response process.

Crisis communication plays a vital role in speedily establishing the initial response plans, therefore this leadership skill assumes greater significance. Communication can be through any available and effective channel. The first level of communication would be with the crisis management team where it is important to convey what is the challenge we are in, what we need to ensure, how we will do it together and what role is expected from each one of them. It is also important to establish a process and channel for continuous two-way communication between the crisis leader and the crisis response team. Although in the thick of activities, it may not always be possible to ensure continuous communication, the leader must make every effort to reach out to the team through the crisis management period.

Crisis communication is a critical enabler for the execution of a well-coordinated response plan and this is one of the most required abilities in a crisis manager. Critical components of crisis communication are accuracy, consistency, succinctness, and timing. A controlled single channel of communication, established on a "need-to-know" basis is the most reliable in a crisis. Multiple and uncontrolled channels tend to result in an information overload, which in the time of a crisis, can be debilitating, as it would take up the crucial time of leaders and the teams and could even lead to wrong decisions being made. In today's world of myriad communication channels and media, the need to establish a single source of truth is extremely important. Accessibility to various digital tools makes this easily achievable. There are proven models of crisis communication frameworks available in the market that are easy to assimilate. Capacity creation in crisis communication and management is a crucial learning requirement that organizations need to integrate with leadership development plans.

An important task of the crisis manager will be the need to manage the environment -which would comprise of the people impacted by the crisis, various stakeholders of the business, the organizational leadership, the public at large and the media. Everyone is anxious to know what is happening and if not properly managed this could become an impediment for the crisis management team to work on the ground. The best way to manage this is to set a process and manage the expectations on when and how updates and information would be shared with others while you are busy managing the situation at hand. The responsibility of sharing accurate pictures about what is happening on the ground can be assigned to the person responsible for a particular response action, however, it is important to ensure such information sharing does not jeopardize the entire response operation.

Another critical element of crisis leadership is that the leader is aware of not just his or her strengths but own anxieties and vulnerabilities. The leader must be able to manoeuvre the negativities within the self, instantly and quickly to be able to stay unfazed in the situation and continue to energize the teams with positivity.

The added responsibility on the shoulders of the leader in a crisis is the task of sharing the bad news with the people impacted and all stakeholders, including the organizational leadership. This is a difficult task and warrants a greater level of emotional restraint and composure on the part of the crisis leader. The crisis manager is required to be clinical in dealing with the situation and the developments around so, the quicker a leader can manage their own emotions, the better would be their ability to lead in a crisis. This personal trait is inherent in many and can be leveraged well and this is further bolstered by lived experiences.

Leading in crisis is a skill developed through a continuous learning process either through personal experiences or case references. Staying focused and assimilating learning in a continuous mode is a critical crisis leadership trait.

2

Case References – Crisis Leadership

CASE 1: COVID-19: UNPRECEDENTED VUCA CRISIS – BUILDING THE PLANE AS YOU FLY

Towards the end of the year 2019, news started trickling in about a hitherto unknown coronavirus outbreak in the city of Wuhan in China. The initial information about the virus and its impact was sketchy. However, as the weeks passed by, more and more information on the origin of the virus and its impact on human lives started emerging, albeit with many contradictory views and confusion about how to deal with this new situation. By the end of January 2020, the World Health Organization (WHO), the leading organization monitoring the evolving situation announced the virus impact as a @public health emergency of global concern@— and the disease was named "Novel Coronavirus-19". In the days that followed, the virus spread to various parts of the world, presumably through travellers who had been to Wuhan since the outbreak of the viral contagion. In a matter of weeks, the virus spread at alarming rates in many countries across the world, and the WHO announced it to be a global pandemic and renamed it COVID-19 – the Corona Virus Disease of 2019.

I was working with an organization operating in the digital ecosystem with a large global footprint. As a member of the global leadership team, my responsibilities included some of the critical internal business-enabling functions. Under this remit, it was my responsibility to gather more information and to update the global leadership about the evolving situation vis-a-vis COVID-19 and its potential impact on our people and business.

Having observed the trend of increasing emergencies over the past few years, we had established a Global Emergency Response Centre (GERC), primarily to track our employees on business travel and support them in emergencies. We quickly added the task of monitoring the COVID-19 situation to the GERC, and a cadence of daily reports to the leadership was established.

This early monitoring enabled us to take many decisive steps, such as restricting global travel, and cancelling participation in many global business events, et cetera, to avoid the risk of exposure to our employees. The situation spiralled to alarming proportions extremely quickly, impacting many countries where our organization had employees. We realized that the time was near when India, where we have the largest employee base, would also be impacted by this pandemic.

At this juncture, based on the discussions among our leadership, it was decided to invoke business continuity plans (BCP), and I was asked to lead the efforts at the global level. Based on identified needs, organizations routinely plan for business continuity under specific disruption scenarios impacting a few locations or people and probably extending for a few days. Continuity and recovery plans for such situations are documented and rehearsed periodically, making it easier to transmit to a business continuity management (BCM) mode from business-as-usual (BAU) and bounce back to normal in the defined period.

The COVID-19 situation was entirely different, as the impact of this pandemic was universal, with no visible time horizon for abatement and life returning to normal. The most critical aspect of this new scenario was the impact on the health and safety of people.

As there was no precedent and no framework to refer to, creating a business continuity protocol for a large organization with employees, customers, and operations spread across many countries, was an enormous responsibility. The speed at which this was required further deepened the complexity and criticality of the efforts. This was a classic VUCA (Volatile, Uncertain, Complex and Ambiguous) situation unfolding.

As the designated leader of the Covid response team with a mandate to prepare a robust response plan, I was facing a huge challenge as to where and how to begin. I had to draw heavily from my learning from past experiences and the first identified requirement was to assemble a very competent and highly motivated team of leaders, who could rally the efforts at this level.

The team was convened immediately with representatives

from various business and shared services units. We started with a call for the cross-functional task (CFT) force with representatives from all the business lines and shared services units. The business heads nominated some of their best leaders for this special task force. A steering committee of global leaders was also convened to provide guidance and support to it. The steering committee and the task force held a series of virtual meetings to discuss and create the approach plan.

Our first critical decision was to lay out the key focus areas for the BCM, which would be driven by the task force. People's safety was recognized as paramount, with business continuity being the outcome. With the objective defined, an array of critical decisions followed, which included the identification of business- or customer-impacting processes, the minimum resources required to perform these, and the locations from where these could be delivered. The need for a documented process to ensure consistency of action was also decided.

The first step was to communicate these decisions to the organizational leadership and all the key stakeholders. Having done this, we set out to create a business continuity document. While this was easy, it soon became evident that with the volatile and ambiguous situation, the identification of risks, Business Impact Analysis (BIA) and their mitigation was not an easy task. This pushed us to deliberate on various possible scenarios that the pandemic could lead us to. We envisaged as many as seventeen scenarios; these, prioritized based on a probability and severity analysis, helped create detailed BCP documents. This hugely challenging task was accomplished within a week with the CFT members and the other stake-holders working round the clock on war footing.

Another challenge we had to combat at this time was the overload of incorrect and misleading information flowing through various social media, causing significant anxiety for the employees. We decided to follow authentic sources of information, such as the World Health Organization and governments across the countries of operation. The GERC was tasked to collate authentic data from these sources and share it with the BCM leadership. A process was established to disseminate the validated information periodically among the employees and other stakeholders.

By the third week of March 2020, the virus contagion in India became a reality. Given the huge population and insufficient healthcare infrastructure, a pandemic of this scale and impact is a serious challenge for a country like India. This prompted the central government to initiate a slew of measures, such as banning international travel, implementing mandatory quarantine for those suspected to have been exposed to the virus, et cetera. The possibility of a national lockdown loomed large.

With over 80 per cent of the employee population and all critical business operations delivered from India, this was a serious situation that was developing around us, and we were cognizant of the impact it could have on our business. The task of the core team now shifted to deciding steps to ensure people's safety and business continuity. The initial approach was a rotational work pattern, with 50 per cent of employees working from the office and the rest from home. While this was being implemented, a national lockdown was declared by many countries, including India.

Transitioning a large workforce to a 100 per cent work-from-home (CFH) scenario was a Herculean task. The biggest challenge was ensuring connectivity and access to the systems for all employees who would work from remote locations. Swift decisions and actions by the Information Technology (IT), supply chain management and facilities teams facilitated moving of desktops to employees' residences and configuring of personal devices for access to systems and tools. The next set of activities included preparing critical facilities from which many processes that could not be addressed remotely could be delivered. This required providing accommodation to these essential resources to stay on-site, this was promptly established by converting some of the office buildings as temporary accommodations with the basic amenities and arrangements for preparing food on site.

We saw the entire transition and arrangements facilitated seamlessly by our support services team. Despite the challenges, many of the contracted support services staff were required to continue to work from the site to keep the operations running. By the time the national lockdown was implemented in India on 23 March 2020, our critical facilities were operational with minimum essential resources, and the rest of the organization had transitioned to work-from-home (WFH) mode.

The need of the hour at this juncture was to devise specific policies to address BCM requirements, such as incentives for those working at sites, home connectivity enablement for those working from home, and so forth. These policies and processes were decided, approved, and implemented on a war footing as and when required.

The CFT members and all other stakeholders worked at amazing speed. All these activities were planned and executed within four days! While at the organizational level, we were ready to ensure business continuity, challenges emerged in continuing with our critical field operations, which is a must to keep the digital network up and running. As a digital infrastructure provider, we are required to manage a colossal fibre network across locations with a field workforce that constitutes a large number of full-term and contractual employees across the globe.

Strangely, in India, the initial government guidelines for essential services that could work during the lockdown did not include our industry! This omission on the part of the administrative agencies became a serious impediment to maintaining network resilience leading to the additional burden of coordination with multiple external agencies to obtain the necessary permissions. This problem was finally overcome by persistent action by our legal team to get the authorities to release necessary amendments to their orders.

By now the BCM core team was a cohesive unit with everyone stretching beyond their remits to take additional responsibility and deliver the required outcomes. There were numerous examples of individuals and teams going above and beyond the call of their normal duties to produce amazing outcomes. We established a cadence of daily reviews with the teams so that immediate support could be extended where required to stabilize the state of BCM.

As the pandemic continued to spread and cause pandemonium across cities and locations, our operations remained steady, with employees remaining safe. End-of-the-year results showed that our employee engagement had remained buoyant; customers were highly appreciative of our support to manage their business continuity and our financial results during the ongoing BCM period were much better than the previous quarters.

This positive outcome despite a major crisis was attributable directly to how the organization responded to the pandemic challenge. The endurance and resilience demonstrated by the organization and specifically the business continuity management team have been exemplary.

"Building a plane as you fly" is not a cliched phrase as practically proven from this crisis management – leaders and teams faced the challenge heads on and forged ahead while fixing the problems and finding the way ahead. This is undoubtedly an exceptional case study of managing crisis, business continuity and delivering positive outcomes in a volatile, uncertain, complex, and ambiguous situation.

Varying facets of organizational resilience, individual traits, leadership qualities and team dynamics were amalgamated into actions and results leading to this sterling achievement. We recognized the need to capture the learning from this unique crisis experience and conducted periodic reflection sessions with the BCM core team members. Significant lessons brought out in these sessions and my own learning as the crisis leader are summarized below:

1. **Delegation and empowerment.** The BCM core team is comprised of nominated members at the senior and middle management levels. Top leadership helped in identifying the right members to be part of this team. Once the team was in place, it was enabled with appropriate empowerment for decisions and actions. These members never had to look back over their shoulders for directions and they acted as fully

empowered battle commanders. The top leadership was easily accessible and available for guidance, support and intervention as and when required.

2. **Seeking and shouldering responsibility.** Each member of the BCM team demonstrated tremendous involvement with the task at hand. Everyone in the team viewed the situation and developments from a larger perspective and stretched beyond their limits to take on additional responsibility to get things moving.

3. **Collaboration.** Seamless collaboration among the teams and at individual levels enabled smooth coordination and completion of activities, leading to quicker turnaround and success. Members of the BCM core team and the extended teams went beyond their functional silos and acted as cohesive teams to resolve critical challenges.

4. **Accountability.** Every member of the BCM core team demonstrated a high level of personal commitment and accountability – both in terms of ensuring the positive outcome as expected and proactively raising flags to resolve constraints that could impact the outcomes negatively.

5. **Communication.** In any crisis, communication plays a vital role to make or mar the outcomes – this assumes greater significance especially in ambiguous situations as was presented by Covid. We recognized this critical aspect in early the stages and spelt out the process for ascertaining the veracity of information, sifting, collating, and disseminating it promptly to all stakeholders. Single point ownership

was assigned to manage communication to a different audience – the Corporate communications team was responsible for communication with customers and external stakeholders, Human Resources owned communication internally within the organization on policies, processes and matters having an impact on employees, Corporate Safety team owned communication on Covid related safety guidelines and BCM team owned communication on operational matters. This facilitated the timely and accurate flow of information leading to the seamless coordination of efforts for initiating and stabilizing BCM and assigning the apprehensions and concerns of employees.

6. **Flexibility.** The BCM core team and the leadership displayed a high level of flexibility to accept and adapt to the rapidly evolving situation. This necessitated modifying and even discarding decisions and plans based on evolving situational requirements. Correspondingly, employees and other stakeholders also demonstrated the flexibility to absorb and adjust to the changes as and when required.

7. **Compassion and sensitivity.** This quality at leadership, individual and team levels is critical in a crisis and assumes greater significance while dealing with situations that impact human safety and lives. The varying nature of the Covid virus infection, lack of a proven treatment methodology, non-availability of medical facilities and increasing death toll across the globe had a severe impact on the mental wellness

of people. This required careful handling of people's problems. It was remarkable that everyone understood this sensitivity and responded to problems involving people empathetically and with utmost care.

8. **Improvising processes.** During a crisis of this nature magnitude and ambiguity, processes related to operations or people management would need to be evolved and improvised continuously. It will be a constant ask on the leaders and crisis managers continuously validate the efficacy of the processes and improvise the same as required and calibrate actions suitably to respond to the evolving situation.

9. **Going Beyond the rule book.** In a crisis of volatile and ambiguous nature, the leaders managing the same would be called upon to respond to the moment in a manner that is not in the standard operating procedure. The ability of the leader to visualize the emergent situation, and evaluate the pros and cons of a decision or action will be a key differentiator. There were many such scenarios during this crisis management period which was brought up for discussions in the BCM core team reviews, one such example was the need to permit our employees to use their personal computing devices to access systems remotely, which was banned as per the information security policy. This decision was taken by the information technology (IT) leadership who did not seem to be limited by the rule books and it resulted in tiding over the significant challenge of a large number of employees not having access to the systems.

CASE 2: COMPASSION IS THE KEY WHEN HORROR UNFOLDS IN THE NEIGHBORHOOD

Mumbai was subjected to one of the worst attacks by terrorists on November 26, 2008. A group of terrorists supported and sponsored by a neighbouring country, covertly entered the southern part of Mumbai city and unleashed mayhem, attacking many iconic landmarks and killing hundreds of innocent people.

I was working with one of India's largest and most respected conglomerates in their newly acquired business unit. My role was to lead the entire gamut of business support services for this global organization. I was based in the office in the Fort area in South Mumbai, with my residence within walking distance at Marine Lines.

On November 26, 2008, after a hectic day's work, I left the office at around 8:45 P.M. On reaching home in about fifteen minutes, I was settling down with a cup of tea when my mobile phone started ringing. The caller was our CEO who informed me that there seemed to be some serious situation in South Mumbai and asked me to check it out on TV. I immediately switched on the TV and saw that many channels were breaking the news about weapons being fired at multiple locations in South Mumbai.

My first action was to contact the police control room immediately, however, this did not succeed. By now, some of the TV channels had started showing visuals of what appeared to be chaos and commotion in and around the area of Colaba. Speculation was that a major inter-gang fight was underway, which is not uncommon in Mumbai. As we continued to watch, some of the channels showed people, many of them bleeding, running out of what looked like hotel lobbies. One could hear incessant gunfire in the background of these visuals. My army background helped me to quickly recognize the continuous buzzing sound of bullets to be from automatic weapons. I called up the CEO to inform him that something serious was happening and that we were checking for more details.

We continued to watch the scenario unfolding on various TV channels. After some time, it was apparent that a major attack had taken place, and that the entire South Mumbai area was in a state of pandemonium. TV channels now carried horrible visuals from two of the premium hotels located in the Colaba and Nariman Point areas, but the details of the incident were still unclear.

As the news developed, the seriousness of the situation became evident. TV channels now showed the impact of the attack and the state of disarray around these areas. My immediate worry was about the situation in our office which is located in the vicinity of these happenings. I called up our head of security, an army veteran (a colonel), who was also staying in the same apartment building as mine. We decided to go to the office immediately. By now, the situation in the area had turned into utter chaos, with thousands of people shouting, screaming and running all over.

As we rushed into our office building, we were confronted by a huge crowd packed into the compound and the lobby of the building. The scene was chaotic, with people jostling, screaming, shouting, and praying loudly.

The security supervisor on duty informed us that they could not prevent the entry of the crowd into our compound as hundreds of people barged into our compound in waves. As we waded through the crowd to reach the reception area on the ground floor of the building, people gathered around both of us, many of them screaming and begging for immediate protection.

Just then, our CEO called on my mobile phone to share an urgent and serious message that one of our senior board members was supposed to be at the Nariman Point hotel, which was under attack, and that his mobile number was not reachable. We were required to check his whereabouts and welfare immediately. We tried to establish contact with the hotel by calling the hotel reception number, but the call did not go through, even after multiple attempts. The situation became very tense, as we were worried about the welfare of the senior person. After some discussion about possible options, the colonel and I decided to go to the hotel, located about fifteen to twenty minutes' walking distance from our office.

As we walked towards the hotel, we could hear continuous clattering of automatic weapons and intermittent explosions. The roads towards the hotel were deserted—on a normal day, this area would be bustling with thousands of people walking in and out of the local railway station at Churchgate.

We walked past the railway station onto Marine Drive, then a police Jeep rushed from behind, overtook and stopped in front of us. A policeman questioned as to who we are and where we were going. Both of us pulled out our ex-servicemen identity cards and explained the details of why we were on the road. The policeman said it was impossible to go near the hotel since it was under siege and all approaches had been barricaded. He also said bullets were hitting the surrounding locality and the roads near the hotel, so it was unsafe for us to venture into that area. We assured him that we would be very careful and take all precautions for our safety and would call off our mission if there was any danger but it was important for us to make the effort to see what was happening, as one of our senior leaders was supposed to be in the hotel under attack.

We continued to walk ahead towards the hotel, applying the tactical movement (moving slowly in a staggered line while observing all around) we had learned in our army days. After about thirty minutes, we managed to reach the Marine Drive promenade on which the hotel is located and reached as close to the hotel as possible. We stood near a police barricade and observed the situation around the hotel. Nothing was visible, as there was a lot of smoke around.

Having realized that it was not possible to get anywhere closer to the hotel, we were trying to figure out the best way to get some information about the people and specifically our senior leader in the hotel. There wasn't much success on this as the situation was chaotic and everyone including the police personnel deployed in the area was also equally confused about the situation. After some time, I called up the CEO to provide an update on these challenges and our inability to get the required information. Fortunately, just before I had called the CEO had received information that our senior leader had not reached the hotel under attack at the time of the incident and was safe at another place. This was a great relief, and we immediately returned to our office.

On reaching back into our office, we observed that the number of people who had taken shelter in the building had increased many fold. There were many foreign nationals among the crowd. Everyone was visibly shaken and scared. It was enormously difficult to manage the huge crowd in the complex. The situation was extremely tense.

Our building was a business-critical facility, and we were anxious that if the terrorists chose to enter our premises after seeing the crowd, it could lead to a major disaster. We were also worried if there was anyone from the attackers' group among the crowd already. The colonel and security team decided to check out the crowd and started to verify the identity and the bags carried by the people and to our relief, we did not find anything which could put our safety at risk. Many people could not show an identity. They were segregated and moved to a separate corner of the compound and kept under strict security watch.

The building also housed some of our critical round-the-clock (24x7) operations, and the employees on duty were worried after seeing the crowd. Many other employees were stranded in the building as they could not travel out due to this sudden and unexpected turn of the events which disrupted the course of normal life. We tasked the security supervisor to go to the office floors and update our colleagues and assure them of safety, while the colonel and I continued to manage the situation on the ground floor.

Among the crowd who had taken refuge in our building was a group of tourists from France. I spoke to them and they narrated their horrible experience. They were planning to enter the Leopold Café located on the causeway in the Colaba area when the terrorists started firing indiscriminately. They ran for their lives and reached the areas of our office building, and seeing many people entering our compound they assumed it was a safe place set up by the authorities and rushed in. By about 11:30 P.M., some of the people from the crowd started moving out of our premises. I suggested to the French tourist group that they should try to go back to their hotel, which was in the same area and offered to organize a vehicle to drop them off. However, they flatly refused and demanded to speak with their diplomatic mission first, which was not possible at that time. We offered the option of moving them to our guesthouse in a nearby building, however, they remained apprehensive and did not agree to move from our building premises.

After many hours of suspense and harrowing experience, the sounds from weapons appeared to be subsiding. The security team who was monitoring TV news updated that police and various other security forces were in action to eliminate the terrorists. The group of French tourists appeared to be a bit relaxed, so we offered them the guesthouse option again. They continued to show reluctance as they felt moving out of the office building would be dangerous. We tried to persuade them to move to the guesthouse, which was a much safer place. They discussed it among themselves for some time and finally agreed to accept the offer to move. Both the colonel and I accompanied the group to our guesthouse, located in a building close by put them up in the rooms, and asked the guesthouse staff to serve them food or refreshments as required. We went back to the office to monitor and manage the situation.

By now the whole picture had become clear; there had been a planned terrorist action at multiple locations in the city, sponsored and orchestrated by our neighbouring country. A fierce gun battle between the terrorists and security forces was continuing in Colaba, Nariman Point, and near the main railway station (CST) and a few other places in the area. Our security command centre was constantly monitoring the situation. I sent out a brief mail to the leadership team on the situation in the area, and the impact on our office facility and employees. From the command centre, we called up the other office facilities in the city to ascertain their status. Fortunately, no other location was impacted, but many employees were stranded in these offices as well. We were trying to ascertain whether any of our employees who could have been outside the office during this attack had been impacted, however, this was not easy in the prevailing circumstances.

The operations by various security agencies, including the police, navy, army and the commandos from the elite National Security Guards continued through the night and the next day in South Mumbai at multiple locations. This part of the city had been completely shut off from the rest; there was no movement of people or vehicles except for emergency services.

Our employees in the office buildings had remained stranded for nearly two days by now and it was an extremely tough task for the support services team to mobilize essential supplies for them.

Throughout the night our CEO was constantly in contact with me. He was concerned about the safety of our employees. Early on 27 November in the morning, he called me to say he would be visiting our Fort office to personally meet our employees. I was not sure about this as the fight between the terrorists and the security forces were continuing in the area and also because the movement of public traffic was completely stopped, it was still not safe to travel by road to this area, so I tried to dissuade him. He, however, persisted and reached our office by about 11 A.M. He reviewed the situation personally, applauded security and other teams who managed the challenging situation on the ground and then went around each floor in a sixteen storied building to meet and talk to every person present in the building. Thereafter he went to other offices as well to repeat the same. This was a huge morale booster for the employees who have been stranded in these offices and those who continued to work tirelessly to keep our operations running, as they could see their CEO reaching out in person without worrying about his safety in such a dangerous situation.

By now, the news about this terrible terror attack had spread across the world. We started receiving calls and emails from employees across the world to check on the condition of our Fort office and the welfare of colleagues. A global employee communication with a succinct situation update was released at this point.

The situation in South Mumbai remained highly tense till the NSG commandos were able to neutralize the terrorists by 28 November after multiple operations. All public activities continued to be low-key for two more days as the forces continued with cleanup operations.

Public activities and life limped back to near normal by November 29, true to the character of Mumbai, a city known to be made of resilient and determined people.

This terrorist attack opened many eyes at the governance level and presented numerous lessons on the management of intelligence and security at the national level. This also turned over an entirely new chapter for corporate security management, especially in public places and luxury hotels. This was a hard wake-up call for lawmakers' administrators and corporations alike. The incident led to the decentralization of NSG, the federal reserve force for counter-terrorism and establishment of NSG hubs in important cities across the nation and the setting up of a new structure for managing intelligence and security agencies at the national level.

This was a completely unexpected situation and a major crisis to manage for the organization. There were many lessons learnt from this lived experience on crisis leadership and team dynamics as enumerated below:

1. **Dealing with ambiguity.** There was absolute confusion as the events started to unfold and for many hours thereafter. Information availability was sketchy, sporadic and unreliable. Putting these pieces of information together to visualize a complete picture of the unfolding situation is an important crisis leadership skill.

2. **Assuming responsibility.** Leaders need to assume responsibility in a developing crisis scenario and personally step up to help manage the crisis on the ground. With hundreds of people barging into the office complex, the outsourced security team was perplexed about dealing with this situation. The head of security reaching out to the location helped them manage the situation properly. Similarly, when there was no reliable information on the developing situation in the hotel where our senior person was presumed to be, the decision to personally visit the hotel is an example of stepping up and assuming responsibility.

3. **Compassion.** With the sound of incessant firing of weapons and blasts around them and with no clear information about the situation people would be scared and extremely worried about their safety, hence they must be treated with empathy. Our approach to facilitating a safe environment for all those who barged into our building complex and providing guesthouse facilities to the tourist group worked well.

4. **Leading from the front.** It is highly motivating when teams witness their leaders on the ground with them in a crisis, especially when it is about dealing with ambiguity and personal safety. While the presence of the security head and myself at the office site was reassuring for the teams; the personal visit by the CEO without worrying about his safety, walking around in the office buildings, and talking with every employee was the most reassuring and motivating factor for our employees.

5. **Respond to immediate tasks as the situation unfolds.** In every crisis, it will be required that the leaders on the ground continuously evolve plans, actions, and responses as the situation unfolds. As the leaders on the ground during this situation, the head of security and I had to address many issues that came up instantly.

6. **Communication.** Like any other crisis, communication played a vital role in managing this crisis. It is important to share the information as available with the stakeholders to obviate the buildup of ambiguity, panic, and resultant action or inaction, which can further aggravate the situation.

CASE 3: EXPECT THE UNEXPECTED – A CRITICAL TRAIT FOR THE CRISIS MANAGER

This crisis occurred in 1989 in Sri Lanka with the Indian Army which I served before joining the corporate sector. I was an officer with an Infantry battalion (referred to as a Unit), deployed as part of the Indian Peace Keeping Force (IPKF). My role (or appointment in military parlance) was that of the adjutant of the unit. I was assigned this role only a few months before this incident. This is one of the key roles in an operational unit that works closely with the commanding officer (CO). An adjutant is a nodal point that links the unit internally and externally with various stakeholders. The role is co-located with the CO at the unit headquarters and is responsible for coordinating the affairs of the unit efficiently on his behalf. The position is, in effect, the "eyes and ears" of the CO. As a general practice, an officer of a captain rank with five-plus years of service is appointed adjutant. For ease of understanding, I will equate the roles of CO and adjutant with that of the CEO and the COO, respectively, in a corporate environment while these army appointments or roles are unique in their characteristics and hence not entirely comparable with the roles or positions in the corporate world.

For a better perspective, let me add the context of the IPKF in Sri Lanka. The deployment of the peacekeeping force was a political decision that unexpectedly transformed into a military conflict with one of the most highly motivated and wily militant groups, the Liberation Tigers of Tamil Eelam (LTTE), which was fighting against the Sri Lankan government for independence of the northern and eastern regions of the country with a majority of Tamil-speaking population. The Indian Army units were deployed in these troubled areas under the peace accord between the Sri Lankan Government and the LTTE, brokered by India. The primary role of the IPKF as defined initially was to disarm the militant groups and help establish peace. The deployment commenced in July 1987. Unfortunately, owing to the then-prevalent political and diplomatic situation, the Indian Army was pushed into an unexpected and unplanned state of combat when the LTTE turned hostile in October 1987. This resulted in a violent fight between the Indian Army and LTTE, lasting over three years in which both sides suffered huge casualties. The Indian Army was particularly at a disadvantage with limited knowledge of the terrain, lack of real-time intelligence on ground realities, and inadequate essential resources, which are critical in any military operation.

This incident narrated here occurred on August 28, 1989. Because of persistent operations by the IPKF from October

1987, the LTTE militants had withdrawn from direct engagement with the Indian Army and had resorted to sporadic activities of violence. Life was near normal for the local citizens, who carried on with their day-to-day activities. The IPKF continued low-intensity operations based on specific information while maintaining a high level of the vigil.

August 28, 1989, was a Monday in the month of Shravan, and as per the Hindu calendar, it had special significance for the troops in my unit. The day is considered auspicious to conduct a special religious ceremony. One of our operational subunits sited away from the HQ had planned to conduct the ceremony, in line with the routines that units followed in operational areas to keep the troops engaged and motivated. An invitation was sent to the commanding officer, which he promptly accepted, as this would be a huge morale booster for the troops.

On the morning of August 28, I briefed the CO on the operational situation as per the daily routine. After breakfast, the CO updated me on his plans to travel to the subunit location to attend the ceremony with the troops. The subunit post to be visited was about six kilometres away from headquarters. As per standard protocol, I alerted the officer-in-charge of the location as well as others along the route and issued orders to the team responsible for such visits to be ready for the move.

Ideally, a "road clearance" procedure—a military drill wherein the road opening patrol (ROP), checks the route for land mines, improvised explosive devices, and possible militant presence and eliminates these risks. Considering the overall situation and it being a day of a festival, the CO decided to allow the troops a day to rest and not to carry out the route clearance drill. This was informed to the officers operationally responsible for the area covering the route to be taken by the CO.

The CO set out as planned at 2 P.M. Typically, the convoy for such visits would consist of two vehicles: one protection vehicle (a Nissan Patrol, known as Jonga in the Indian Army, a sturdy vehicle with a powerful engine) with a mounted machine gun that moves in front, followed by the CO's vehicle, a Jeep. He would normally be accompanied by a radio operator and one protection person in his vehicle in addition to the driver. This visit was a special occasion, the subedar major (the senior-most officer in the ranks of personnel below officers) was also accompanying the CO. For that trip, the CO decided to drive Jonga himself. Under normal circumstances, the distance to the location from the HQ would have been covered in about forty-five minutes, so the CO and his team were expected to reach the planned destination by about 2:45 P.M.

After seeing him off at the HQ gate, I decided to go around the locality to check the alertness of the troops deployed on the posts and to do some "gup-shup" (military parlance for light conversation) with the troops. This gup-shup routine is a huge morale booster for the troops deployed in a warlike situation in an alien country. I must have spent about twenty-five minutes walking around and chatting with the troops when the office runner (a person designated to carry documents and messages) came rushing and calling out loudly for me. His body language and the anguish in his voice conveyed a sense of tragedy. Thoughts started buzzing in my mind—was there a mine blast, an attack on an outpost, or an encounter with militants? What could have happened?

I dashed back to the control room and grabbed the field telephone handset. From the other side, I heard the voice of the officer-in-charge of the area on the route taken by the CO, who crisply said, "The CO has been ambushed, and I am rushing with the quick reaction team [QRT] to the site. Updates will follow." We quickly decided to activate the wireless communications, which was not permitted under the "radio silence" order, to avoid leakage of information, as the LTTE was found to be monitoring it. Revoking radio silence required permission from the higher HQ; however, under the circumstances, it would have caused delays, so between the two of us, we decided to go ahead with the use of wireless sets. Many chilling thoughts rushed through me, and my feet froze. By now, the news had spread in the unit HQ building, and anxious people gathered around the control room.

For a few moments, I was overwhelmed by the enormity of this unprecedented situation and the task at hand. Firstly, I needed to ascertain what had happened and coordinate the required support operations. Secondly, as the adjutant and the only officer in the unit HQ, it was my responsibility to keep the higher HQ informed about the incident, and thirdly, I had to alert the units near the encounter site and, most importantly, assuage the concerns of the troops around me. The information at this point was incomplete and not enough for me to address any of these instant tasks. I tried to attempt wireless contact with the area officer, who had gone to the encounter site with the quick reaction team, but there was no response. We then tried calling the CO's radio operator; there was no response from him either. The ambiguity continued to loom large—I did not know what had happened, where, how, and what was the damage. Each second passed like an eternity. In a few minutes, a fleeting thought about those who were at the actual ambush site arose, and I realized that I was in a much better position and that it was on me to take the required action to support them. This thought pushed me out of my shock inertia.

After multiple attempts, we were able to connect on the landline with another subunit along the same route. We got a vague idea about the location of the incident and were told that the CO's convoy had been attacked by militants and there were many casualties. I could see the news hitting the men around me like a sledgehammer. I was deeply shocked upon hearing this news but tried to regain my composure as I saw the drooping faces and shoulders around the room. All I could say was, "Yes, the CO has been ambushed. Details are not known. But everything will be fine...all of you, do not worry and go back to your seats." I requested one of the senior people to take care of them.

I had to get on with the next difficult task of informing the higher headquarters and asked the telephone operator to connect me to the brigade major (BM; an appointment at the higher HQ similar to that of the adjutant in the unit). The HQ operator said that the BM was in a meeting with the brigade commander. I urged the operator that the matter was extremely serious and that I must be connected immediately. Disturbing a senior commander engaged in a meeting is not in line with the army protocol, hence the operator was reluctant, however as I persisted with the demand, he put me through to the commander's office, and the office assistant of the commander answered the call. I quickly introduced myself and asked him to connect me with the BM urgently. After some time, the BM came online.

I told the BM, as quickly, crisply, and calmly as I could, "Sir, our CO has been ambushed somewhere around the area [reference to the map location was made], but I do not have any more details at this point. We have sent out a QRT, which is on the way. I will revert with more details as soon as I have them." I also informed him about our revoking radio silence and quickly put the phone down. The BM was not happy with this.

By now, about ten minutes would have passed from the time we had received the first information about the incident. We tried to establish contact again on the wireless sets to gather some information, but there was no response. In the meantime, we received many calls from the Brigade HQ asking for more updates. I did not attend all the calls and directed the telephone operator to give a standard answer to all callers "adjutant saheb bahut busy hain, weh app ko call back karenge" (adjutant is very busy and he will call you back).

The state of ambiguity and apprehension continued and every second of waiting appeared to be an eternity. After some time, suddenly the wireless set crackled with the voice of the QRT commander, who said, "The CO is safe; unfortunately, his driver has been killed, and there are a few more casualties. I am moving them to the field hospital." I immediately called up the BM to update him on the available details about the incident. He wanted more about the circumstances as to how the incident occurred and also wanted an update about what operations have been initiated to eliminate the militant group responsible for the ambush. I had no idea about the operations at this time, so my answer again was, "I will come back to you with the details, sir."

Just then, to our great relief, we heard the voice of the CO on the radio set. He asked for me and briefly narrated the sequence of events; it was amazing that even after surviving an ambush of this magnitude, the CO was calm and composed. I updated him that I have informed the brigade headquarters and there are many questions from them to know more about the incident and follow-up operations taken up by us. The CO told me that he would directly speak to the brigade commander to provide all required updates.

What followed thereafter was a hectic series of activities. There were many actions to be coordinated, firstly with the field hospital for the care of the wounded soldiers who have been evacuated there, secondly with the safe movement of the CO back to our HQ, and also coordination with the subunits of my battalion and other similar units in the neighbouring areas to launch immediate cordon-and-search operations to capture or eliminate the militants. As the adjutant, I also had to send out formal communication in writing, to the brigade HQ and other units deployed in the neighbouring areas.

The CO asked me and the company commander in the area of the incident to plan the follow-up operation with other units and subunits, coordinate the execution and keep him and the HQ informed about the progress. Execution of the follow-up operation was influenced by many factors, such as the militants' ability to disappear quickly with the support of locals, terrain constraints, time passed from the occurrence of the incident and the need to mobilize additional troops required to cover the entire areas making it extremely challenging. We needed to move quickly. The cordon and search operations were launched as fast as we could, and they continued throughout the night and the following day, covering the entire area.

For an army unit deployed in any operational area, an encounter with adversaries is a major incident that needs to be handled deftly and speedily. If the incident involves the life and safety of the commanding officer, who is the head of the unit, the significance is much higher, and the responsibility of handling such a situation is enormous.

In this incident, I was the person responsible for making critical decisions and coordinating many crucial actions. Although I had been through many challenging operational situations while deployed in Sri Lanka, this was an entirely different scenario. Honestly, I was initially confused with a nagging apprehension that something serious involving the life of the Commanding Officer had occurred. This sense of apprehension pushed me to a state of confusion, however, the enormity of the responsibility nudged me to overcome this state of inertia and coordinate actions as described. This state of confusion and inertia would be natural for anyone in a similar kind of situation, however, the key is to realize that the sooner one overcomes this mental and physical state, the better it would be. The highest level part of army service is that one can be assured of the highest level support from the unit, under all circumstances. This awareness strengthened my resolve to face the situation with a sense of determination and conviction. In the subsequent reviews and debriefings that followed, the way this challenging situation was handled and responded to was acknowledged and applauded by the CO and the higher HQ.

Many important observations and conclusions were drawn from this incident in the subsequent reviews and debriefing, as per the standard process in the army. At a personal level, I can say that this incident laid the foundation for building my resilience and provided me with the impetus to deal with many other crises that I had to deal with in my long professional career.

Key lessons that I could imbibe from this crisis experience are enumerated below:

1. **Be prepared for the "unexpected".** Leaders need to stretch their imagination beyond the obvious while planning. Multiple scenarios, including the worst case, need to be visualized. Being anticipative would aid in being mentally prepared for the unexpected. There is no singular method to predict what exactly would happen in a crisis, especially in a conflict scenario as narrated in this lived experience. In th hindsight the conclusion was that if we could have spent more time reviewing and planning the travel by road in a conflict zone, the possibility of such an act by the militants could have been visualized and, the precautionary measures such as the road opening drill and additional protection for the team moving on the road could have been put in place.

2. **Keep calm amid unnerving ambiguity in a crisis of this nature,** with truly little information about the incident and its aftermath, it is natural for one to become apprehensive and pessimistic. The challenge for the leader in this situation would be to mask the

personal anxieties and continue to perform the expected role as a leader.

3. **Communication.** In a crisis, everyone outside the situation wants instant information. In an evolving incident, the facts and details emerge as the situation unfolds. The leader in the situation may not always have adequate or accurate information and would also be pressed for time. It is therefore important to garner all the information and inputs available and prepare crisp communication- Accuracy, brevity, clarity, and timing (A, B, C, and T) are the keys to effective crisis communication. The army has standard procedures and formats for all types of communications. In the corporates where a proper procedure for crisis management exists such formats would be available, where it does not the need will be to ensure communication is properly planned and managed.

4. **Leave people in the thick of things free.** In a crisis, everybody is in a state of flux. It is imperative to allow time for them in the thick of the situation to do their part. Therefore, for interested parties outside the crisis-impacted area, patience is the key. The biggest worry that occupied my mind throughout the situation narrated here, was how to respond to the frequent calls from HQ for updates.

5. **Empower your mind; you are not alone.** Situations, when a leader is all alone to deal with a crisis, are decisive moments for personal grit. The leader needs to relate himself to those present in the real crisis and are in a much worse situation than the leader himself, it will evoke self-assurance and confidence. The

fleeting thought about the CO and others at the ambush site as compared to me in the safe environment of the headquarters, provided me with the required stimulus for positive thinking and to initiate the actions expected of me as the crisis leader. One needs to reassure oneself and empower the mind to assume the challenge in such situations and these are the rarest and best opportunities for forging personal resilience.

3

Crisis Leadership Summary

A crisis leader, whether by the role assigned or impromptu nominated in a situation, carries tremendous responsibility on the shoulders. Leadership plays a critical role in the outcome of the crisis response and management. Even if one is a crisis manager by role and has been fully trained on the defined crisis management processes, when faced with a real crisis it is possible that one is mentally not in the right space and doesn't have the confidence to deal with the situation. In such scenarios what enables the leader is the ability to overcome these insecurities with the power of determination. There would be many conflicts within your mind, which need to be mastered within the shortest available time. As a leader one cannot afford to be seen as tentative. The most important requirement is that the leader needs to be in control of themselves, only then you can control the situation around them.

Critical thinking is an important leadership trait that helps to deal with a crisis. The leader needs to actively think, analyze systematically and take the most appropriate decisions. Once a decision is taken, the leader needs to stand by it, continuously monitor the evolving crisis and modify decisions and actions as warranted to suit the developments on the ground.

Another key factor that plays out in the corporate sector is a higher degree of empowerment and enablement, which allows the freedom and flexibility to make decisions and access resources as would be required. The military practice of empowering leaders on the ground and allowing them to decide and act appropriately with the evolving situation around them applies equally in a corporate environment as well. Senior leaders need to step back, observe and step up only where required to supplement the team's ability to quickly deal with a particular situation or action that might have a critical impact on the overall outcome. They must be constantly available and accessible, yet not interfere with the freedom of the leader managing the situation. The role of the senior leadership will also be to guarantee the availability of all the resources required to manage the situation from across various sources, internally and externally. A sense of assurance in the minds of the crisis leader and team at the forefront of the crisis will have a significant impact on their confidence and consequential influence on the outcomes.

Practical experiences would affirm that the most vital characteristic that ignites the ability to act in a unified manner in any crisis is mutual trust—an environment wherein the team members align themselves well with their roles and are confident about the abilities of other members and, most importantly, their leader. Leadership traits such as professional competence, fairness, flexibility, and the ability to lead from the front add up significantly towards this and makes a positive impact on the team. Conversely, the leader also should know and believe that the team is competent, motivated, and committed to facing up to challenges posed by any crisis. In a corporate environment, there is no characteristic organizational fabric, as it is in the Army that inspires mutual trust naturally, and thus it becomes an added responsibility of the corporate leaders to create and nurture an environment that fosters a sense of trust. There is no magic wand to achieve this state of mutual trust and respect and leadership charisma alone cannot do much. An environment of mutual trust gets built over some time with consistent efforts and deliberations as teams and leaders work together. The foundation of this is laid even in business-as-usual conditions when dealing with routine operational challenges in the process.

Salient leadership traits and principles based on the practitioner's experience of leading in crisis, as highlighted in the case references narrated in this book are:

1. **Know yourself:** As a leader when confronted by a crisis your choice is limited to responding to the need of the hour in the most appropriate manner. What would drive a leader in such scenarios would be the three Cs of crisis management – Curiosity, Compassion and Courage. The situation may be volatile, uncertain, complex and ambiguous but your abilities to decide and act swiftly, and motivate the teams and people around you are what will stand you in good stead. Knowing yourself is a process of continuous introspection and reflection and building

on what is deficient or strengthening that is inherent in you.

2. **Trust the ability of the team:** The leader's ability or confidence does not alone enable successful management of a crisis – it largely depends on what and how the crisis management team does in such scenarios. It is possible that the leader would need to work with a completely unknown team. Curiosity and a quick learning mindset would help the leader to understand the team. The leader needs to have complete confidence in the ability of the team to deal with the situation and facilitate an environment of confidence and positivity that keeps the team engaged with the task at hand.

3. **Think on your feet:** In a dynamically evolving situation, the crisis leader would be required to make decisions on the spur of the moment, hence the need to be hands-on with the developments and anticipate continuously on what could emerge next. The leader needs to have the ability to see beyond the obvious and visualize possible scenarios and responses.

4. **Let Go:** "Everything through me" is not a desired leadership style even in a business-as-usual scenario. This assumes greater significance in a crisis. Empowerment and enablement are critical outcome enablers. Leaders need to be aware of when to let go and allow the team in action to take decisions and manage them in consonance with the dynamically evolving situations in a crisis.

5. **Manage your resources prudently:** This is very critical as one cannot estimate how a crisis scenario

would unfold and how the resources would get consumed. The leadership should be able to continually assess the evolving situation and assess the need for material and human resources. Deployment and commitment of these need to be prudently managed, lest one land in a situation bereft of the required wherewithal.

6. **Identify and define the objectives:** Based on the nature of the crisis and its impact on people and business. The ability to quickly calibrate the objectives in line with the evolving situation or unexpected development that may emerge in a long crisis scenario is a critical leadership requirement.

7. **Establish clear channels and ownership for communication:** The outcomes from a crisis management scenario can be significantly impacted by communication. This is required within the crisis management teams horizontally and vertically, for the larger organization internally and the stakeholder ecosystem externally.

8. **Lead from the front:** In situations of uncertainty and chaos, the visibility and accessibility of the leader play a vital role in keeping people engaged, motivated and in a positive mindset. The leader needs to be with the team through the thick and thin of the crisis. It may not be possible to be physically present in a crisis always, however remaining in constant communication with the team in crisis, proactively enabling mobilization of resources and being patient, tolerant, empathetic and considerate when the chips are down, will certainly enable the teams to stay positive,

motivated and focused to manage the crisis and emerge successful. This does not mean every action needs to be micromanaged– a leader must allow the team to decide what is best within the overall crisis management framework and be empowered to modify plans and actions as suited to the situation around them

9. **Own your decisions:** In a crisis, many people look up to the leader for decisions. It is possible that the leader does not have all the required information and most importantly the luxury of time to make decisions. The leader would still need to take decisions and ensure it translates to actions as required to manage the crisis. Certain decisions may likely deliver positive outcomes, but the leader needs to have the dexterity to identify the problem and take fresh decisions as required. Owning the decisions when things go wrong is the most important leadership trait that helps build positivity and continued trust in a crisis scenario.

10. **Remember the basics:** The team leading the crisis are under constant stress. The situation could be so demanding that the team members are not in a position to take care of their basic personal needs. The leader needs to ensure logistic support for food and rest is established and maintained throughout to enable the well-being of the team, especially in a prolonged crisis.

11. **Record and share Learning:** Each crisis is a unique opportunity that enables tremendous learning which will help develop crisis response plans and

management for the future. It is therefore important to conduct a debriefing session after managing the crisis, wherein an objective analysis of the end-to-end scenarios, responses, constraints and mitigations are discussed threadbare. Innovative ideas implemented and successful process enhancements implemented during the crisis need to be reviewed and formalized. Experience sharing by each member must be encouraged. This learning should be compiled and published for the benefit of all stakeholders. Corrective and preventive measures identified during the process should be implemented within a defined timeline.

Leading in crisis is a critical leadership skill. The mechanics to deal with a crisis can be learnt from theory and mastered through practice such as desktop exercises and mock drills under business-as-usual scenarios. However the acid test will be during an actual crisis scenario, wherein the interplay of innate leadership traits and learned skills translates to demonstrated performance of the leader. The critical qualities that a leader displays in a crisis are the manifestations of conscious and unconscious learning over some time, characterized by the basic leadership ability at the individual level. The leader needs to focus on honing individual leadership skills continually through the process of training and reflecting on their own experiences of managing crises. Learning from the experiences shared by others can stimulate the thought process and the ability to draw from one's reservoir of experience.

SPACE FOR READER'S REFLECTIONS

....

....

....

....

....

....

....

....

....

....

....

....

....

....

....

....

....

....

....

....

SECTION 2

Team Dynamics in Crisis Management

Conflicts Build Character ... Crisis Defines It.

—**Steven V Thulon**

4

How Teams Work in a Crisis

The previous chapter highlighted the importance of crisis leadership and many of the critical leadership skills required to successfully lead in a crisis, as extruded from the lived experiences narrated. Success in crisis management, however, is not just about leadership. The best leadership cannot alone achieve positive outcomes in managing a crisis without the action and contribution of a motivated and cohesive team. Building this unified team and orchestrating their actions to deliver the expected outcome in a crisis, is therefore yet another significant crisis leadership challenge.

Undeniably, the team is the most critical enabling factor for the successful management of a crisis. In the normal course of enterprise risk management, for a pre-assessed event with a documented response plan, a team comprising identified and nominated members would be available. However, in the event of an unprecedented and unexpected crisis, a new team would need to be created in consonance with developing the response plan itself. If a pre-assigned team is available, this task would be easier as it calls for augmenting the capacity of the existing team by coopting additional members from different work streams as warranted by the specific crisis. However, building a new team from scratch would be a significant management challenge, where such a plan does not exist for any kind of crisis response.

Building a crisis response team in the hour of need and keeping it cohesive, engaged and motivated to see through the entire crisis management period is one of the many challenges that the leadership needs to deal with at the beginning of a crisis. The immediate task of the person assigned the role of the crisis leader would be to ascertain the composition of the team. The composition of the crisis management team would vary depending on the nature of the crisis and the response mechanism to be established to eliminate the business risk emerging from the crisis. Speed of decision and action is extremely important at this initial stage. A crisis management team would usually be comprised of representatives from various business and support functions and making this effective in the quickest time will be a real challenge. The crisis leader would be called upon to shoulder this responsibility of getting the members with the right ability and attitude to be part of this cross-functional task force so that there are positive team dynamics that enable the desired outcomes.

For this narrative, the broader definition of the term "team dynamics" is the functional and behavioural interplay between the team members while working together to achieve the defined goals for the crisis management team.

After forming a cross-functional team, the foremost task of the crisis leader would be to bring the team up to speed and ensure they are fully abreast with the emerging situation. The leader would need to clearly articulate the purpose of the crisis management team and the specific business objectives to be ensured or achieved. The next step would be for the crisis leader to define the broader operational framework for the crisis management team and within that the role to be played by each of the cross-functional team members. The role and responsibility of each of the team members would differ from what they have been doing in a business as a usual mode of operations. The operational standards and deliverables in a crisis would also be different from the routine job role. Therefore, it is imperative that the roles are clearly defined and assigned appropriately, aligned with the skills and capabilities that each of the team members brings to the table and the expected deliverables are delineated and stated clearly.

A defined working structure for the crisis management team is essential to avoid overlaps, duplication of efforts and dilution of ownership. This further underlines the need for role clarity within the crisis management team. With clearly delineated roles it becomes easy for the crisis leader to monitor the actions and progress of the crisis response plan and extend support where required. The structure also makes it easy to delegate authority at critical junctures to facilitate quicker decisions and actions in-situations as warranted by the evolving situation. This further bolsters the sense of empowerment for the subordinate crisis leaders and team members motivating them to deliver the best efforts.

Effective working and positive team dynamics in a crisis

71

response team are also enabled by a structured communication plan. Crisis by nature is ambiguous, hence a robust communication process within the team horizontally and vertically is the key enabling factor for successful crisis management. It is the responsibility of the crisis leader to defining how continuous two-way communication needs to be ensured within the team. The process for periodic check-ins and the frequency of situation update reports must be defined upfront. The plan should also build in enough flexibility to facilitate quicker communication based on urgencies in a critical situation. It is also vital to develop redundancies in the communication plan to avoid a total breakdown in communication at critical junctures of crisis management. There is an array of technology solutions available today such as mobile phones, low-range walkie-talkie sets, application-based crisis management tools and emails to manage crisis communication most efficiently and reliably. The crisis leader would be required to make the right choice of one or a combination of many modes of communication to best suit the situation to be dealt with.

Conflicts are bound to arise when a crack task force comprising members from different parts of the organization, who would never have worked together under the Business-as-Usual scenario, come together to deal with a crisis. Differences of views and opinions to evaluate response options or decisions are desirable. However, if differing views lead to a clash of personalities impacting actions, it will be detrimental to the process of crisis management. Such conflicts if not resolved can have far-reaching impacts on crisis management outcomes. Conflicts of this nature can be reduced to a great extent by providing clarity on the roles, responsibilities and the process for resolving overlaps and ambiguities, right at the beginning when the operating framework for the crisis management team is being established. However, a crisis by its nature is characterized by evolving and unknown situations which can potentially create a conflict within the team. The leader, therefore, needs to recognize the fact that conflicts cannot be completely ruled out. Where such conflicts arise during the action, the leader would be required to expeditiously ascertain the facts, analyze objectively, identify the root cause and facilitate constructive debate within the time constraints and provide guidance to resolve the differences before it impacts the overall performance of the task force.

At the personal level, whether as a crisis leader or as a crisis team member, the traits essential to foster positive dynamics within the task force remain constant. These are adaptiveness, flexibility, open-mindedness, ability to listen, willingness to accept suggestions and patience. The crisis leader's role calls for the ability to identify and ignite these traits in the team members.

Striving through any crisis is not about one individual; it is pure team play and this can be achieved only if the team dynamics are positive. Strong crisis leadership is an important catalyst to promote positive team dynamics. The crisis leader has the responsibility to engage with each of the individual team members and evoke the best behaviour from them leading to the highest level of positive response and action. The leader needs to be alive to the unfolding scenarios, and appreciate the challenges and ambiguities the crisis response team has to deal with. The leader needs to facilitate access and availability of the required resources and logistical support to the team. When required the leader would need to roll up their sleeves and get into the action with the team. This kind of demonstrated crisis leadership will ignite a positive energy in the team who will identify the leader as one among them – rather than someone managing or controlling remotely. This will also help foster better understanding and coordination among the team members, which is crucial for the success of crisis management. The crisis leader should continuously strive to create and foster an atmosphere of trust and confidence in the team which leads to positive and impactful team dynamics – and for this one does not have the luxury of time in a crisis scenario.

In every crisis, there will be individuals who will rise above and beyond the call of their regular duty to accomplish astounding results. These singular acts of exceptional performance would motivate other team members and bolster the collective resolve of the team to push their limits to achieve positive outcomes. As reflected in the narrated experiences in this book, even in a disparate corporate environment, challenging crises do stimulate remarkable positivity and people demonstrate a determined level of response beyond the call of their regular duties.

Managing a crisis calls for moral and physical courage. Moral courage is the ability to act for moral reasons despite the potential negative outcomes. Physical courage is the ability to face physical hardships including risks to own life Courage is an outcome of both nature and nurture. The military is a good example of this – people are selected based on a personality assessment and physical strengths and further imparted training uniformly to augment the characteristics of courage. This process of selection and training brings out the best of individual and collective actions in times of adversity, which is the purpose and mainstay of the military. In a corporate environment, there is no such standardized assessment process to determine the personality type at the time of hiring and there is no training program focused on developing the individual traits required to manage a crisis, as it is not the main organizational purpose. Therefore, for the crisis leader, it becomes an added responsibility to ensure that the crisis management team stays aligned with the defined purpose, and is ready to face the situation even if it is extremely challenging with risk to personal safety.

A team that exudes positive dynamics with confidence, mutual trust, risk appetite and tenacity, led by a capable crisis leader will be truly motivated to deal with and surpass a crisis, irrespective of its nature and severity. From my experience of managing different crisis scenarios with diverse challenges, it is well evidenced that teams, whether pre-assigned, trained or built on the need of the hour will deliver astonishing performance in the face of challenges, even in a corporate environment, with the leadership that fosters a positive team dynamics.

5

Case References – Team Dynamics in Crisis Management

CASE 1: THE LEADER IS AS GOOD AS THE TEAM ON THE GROUND

Following an eventful tenure of over a decade in the Indian Army, I sought premature voluntary retirement and was released in January 1995. After an initial stint in the corporate sector with an IT services organization in Mumbai, I accepted a job with a large business conglomerate in the Sultanate of Oman in 1998. At the time of this incident, I was a senior manager in the human resources and administration (HR&A) department of this organization, reporting to the group manager for the HR&A.

On the morning of a day in June 2000, I had gone to the airport to receive my family, who were returning from a holiday in India. We left the airport at around 8:30 A.M., and while driving back on the highway, my mobile phone started ringing. Initially, I ignored it but when the caller persisted, I pulled over, stopped the car, and took the call. The caller was a key person in the organization, and it was not normal for him to call me at that time of the day.

When I acknowledged the call, the caller showed great urgency and said there had been a serious accident at the residence of one of our senior leaders (for the story, we will refer to him as L.D.) and as a result, one of the house staff had suffered severe injuries. The caller wanted me to immediately reach the incident site to handle the situation and support L.D. In the normal course, for such an incident my supervisor would have been called, but it could not be done as he was away from the country on vacation.

After finishing the call, I decided to go straight to L.D.'s, house, which was about forty-five minutes of driving distance from my location. As I continued to drive on, I received the information that the accident victim had been moved to a nearby hospital. I changed my destination to reach the hospital. As my family was still with me in the car, I waved down a taxi to send them home.

As I reached the hospital, I saw L.D. standing near the casualty and emergency ward in a state of shock and distress. I quickly took a brief about the accident. The circumstances leading to the accident seemed complicated. As per the standard procedure in such cases, the hospital administration informed the police, and they arrived soon and started with their procedures.

At this point, I realized the need to have a person conversant with the local language and procedures to be with me, who can ensure effective communication and coordination with the police and local authorities.

To understand the complexity of managing this crisis, it is important to share the peculiarities of the work environment in the Middle East. The majority of the workforce comprises expatriates largely from Asian countries. People take up jobs in the middle eastern countries with a narrow and short-term focus essentially because of the higher salary levels offered as compared to their home countries. Organizations are mostly proprietary and managed through rigid hierarchical structures. A potpourri of cultural backgrounds, work ethics, and languages aggravate the challenges of building cohesive teams. The rigid hierarchical structure and huge power wielded by the top managers encourages a tendency for everyone to focus on the people at the top level. Mutual trust is at the lowest levels and non-existent at times between the layers of organizational hierarchy and among the functional teams, leading to frequent conflicts. Creating a positive team dynamic is an extremely difficult proposition in this environment.

To further add to this complicity, I was not number one in the function when called upon to handle this situation and therefore was apprehensive of the challenges, especially mobilizing support from others, as would be required to manage this crisis.

The working language at the office was English, however, to deal with the government authorities knowledge of the local language (Arabic) was essential. For this purpose, a local citizen is appointed as the public relations officer (PRO), in all business organizations. The PRO in my organization was functionally reporting to my manager and my interaction with him at work was limited thus there wasn't a great rapport with him. Given the situation that I was in, I had no option but to call up the PRO and request he to come to the hospital immediately. To my surprise, the PRO was quick in understanding the gravity of the situation and responded positively. He reached the hospital shortly after and then accompanied the police and L.D., to the accident site to conduct the investigations. I continued to remain at the hospital, closely interacting with the doctors attending to the accident victim and other officials.

At around 2 P.M., one of the doctors informed me that the accident victim's condition was deteriorating. Immediately, I called up L.D., but he could not be reached as his mobile phone was switched off. At about 3 P.M., the doctors informed me that the victim had succumbed to the injuries. I called L.D. again on his mobile phone but could not reach him, so I called up on the landline at his residence. The person who picked up the call said L.D. had left the residence with the police a few minutes earlier. I was not sure whether they were headed to the hospital or going elsewhere as part of the investigation. I waited for about ten to fifteen minutes (approximate driving time from L.D.'s residence to the hospital.) When no one turned up, I decided to go to the police station. On reaching the police station, I saw L.D. and our PRO sitting with the police officer. I shared the news about the sad demise of the accident victim with them. With the death of the accident victim, the case now became more complicated, and the police officer wanted to visit the hospital again.

By now, the news had reached various levels of management in the organization, and I started receiving several calls seeking information about the accident and the latest updates. Owing to the stature of L.D. in the organization, the entire proceedings were being monitored closely by the senior management. A high level of sensitivity was required to handle the situation.

At the hospital, the police questioned the emergency ward staff and doctors and checked various documents and medical records of the victim. They wanted to ascertain more facts from L.D. to rule out any suspicion about the circumstances leading to the accident and death. While this was happening, we had to initiate the next set of activities of getting the mortal remains released from the hospital and dispatching it further to the victim's home country, Ethiopia.

The procedure to send the mortal remains to the home country opened another series of complexities. As per local law, a clearance certificate from the diplomatic mission of the country of the deceased is mandatory for the repatriation of human remains. Ethiopia, the home country of the deceased person did not have a diplomatic mission in Oman, and the nearest was in Saudi Arabia. This would entail a protracted process of submitting various forms and documents explaining the details of the accident and the victim. There could be clarifications sought by the officials at the diplomatic mission before they issued the clearance certificate. To further add to this complication, the day the incident occurred was a Wednesday, leaving just one working day before the weekend closure as Friday is the weekend in the Middle East. If the required paperwork was not completed on Thursday, it would lead to the process being postponed till Saturday, the next working day and possible further delays in completing the formalities.

While I was overwhelmed by the situation and all the work to be done, I soon realized that my apprehensions were misplaced. My manager, although away from the country on a vacation, was continually available on phone for guidance and support as required. The PRO was an experienced person who proactively assumed the responsibility to coordinate with the police, hospital, and other authorities. He also pitched in to answer queries from various people in the organization. The PRO, on his initiative, added another member to the team, the legal assistant in our office who was a Sudanese national and thus proficient in the local language and procedures. This new team member was assigned the task of coordination with the diplomatic mission in Saudi Arabia.

Once we started the process of document submission to the diplomatic mission, we realized it was a lot more difficult than what he had assessed. The first challenge was to establish the initial contact. After repeated attempts over the telephone, we were able to contact them by around 4:30 P.M., only to be told that the office hours were over. On our persistent pleading, the person at the other end of the phone call agreed to receive a fax message with the case details. He said the details will be reviewed by the relevant officials and they would try to revert as quickly as possible over fax message. The case summary was sent by fax from our end immediately with the required supporting documents. It was about 6.30 P.M. by the time this activity was completed. Hoping for quick action on this request by the diplomatic mission we waited till about 9 PM, however, there were no responses and telephone calls went unanswered, so we called off the activity for the day.

Being anxious about the response from the diplomatic mission and with worries about getting the procedures completed in just a day, we reached our office early morning the next day. The first action was to rush to the fax machine expectantly, only to realise to our dismay, that no message had come in from the diplomatic mission. Normal working hours start at 8 A.M. in this part of the world and we had no other option but to wait, to make a telephone call to follow up on the clearance certificate.

We were able to get through to the mission over the telephone by about 9:30 A.M. This time there was a different official on the other side of the phone and the entire situation had to be explained all over again. This person informed us that the official authorized to issue a clearance certificate of this nature was not available at this time. We were advised to wait for the procedure to get completed till about 11:30 A.M.

This development further heightened our tension. Although the cargo had been booked, the airline would confirm it only after all the permissions were in place and the cut-off time to submit all papers to the airline was 2 P.M. Any delay in submitting the documents would mean that the airline will cancel the booking, jeopardizing the entire plan.

With no news coming from the diplomatic mission by 11:30 AM, we called them up again, to be told that given the nature of the accident, a police report was required, for review. They informed us that the clearance would be subject to the case details mentioned in the police report. Our PRO rushed to the police station with the hope of procuring the certificate quickly, however, he was told that such a report to a diplomatic mission can only be released after clearances from their senior officers. It took multiple calls to various officials by our PRO to get the report issued by around 12:30 P.M. Now, we had only an hour and a half to obtain the clearance from the diplomatic mission and then pass that onwards to the airline. This was a race against time.

Finally, the certificate as required by the police was received it was sent to the diplomatic mission via fax instantly. Our legal assistant kept calling up the mission, over and over again, much to their annoyance. After repeated follow-up and pleading, received the clearance letter was finally via fax by 1:30 P.M., which was further transmitted to the airline office – just in time enabling us to complete the documentation formalities before the deadline at 2 P.M.

With all the arrangements for dispatching the mortal remains in place, the next task was to coordinate the collection of the mortal remains at Addis Ababa. This called for sharing this sad news with the family. From the victim's documents, we learnt that a sibling had worked with an organization in the past. With the contact details available in our records, we called up the person.

Breaking the news about death is an extremely difficult task for anyone at any time. Although I had the experience of handling similar situations during my army service, I was apprehensive owing to the peculiarities of this incident. The information to be shared here was about an accident and death of a very young person which the family would not have been expecting. Another limitation here was the language constraint for me if I were to break this sad news.

We leveraged the expertise of our legal assistant, to draft a short script in English and Arabic. The plan was that I would initiate the call in English and then hand over the phone to the legal assistant, who would convey more details in Arabic.

The time difference between Muscat and Ethiopia was only 1.5 hours behind our local time, so it was not an odd time to call. The number available in the personal records was that of a landline phone and it took multiple attempts to get through. I initiated the conversation as planned and asked for the sibling who had worked with us in the past. The person was not available at that time, so we said we would call back in some time and requested the availability of the sibling. We called back after one hour and the sibling with whom we had planned to share the news was available. As soon as I mentioned the name of the victim, I got an enthusiastic response that they were waiting for the person to be home on holiday soon. I continued most somberly as I could and read out the English part of the script and extended my condolences. After that I handed over the phone to our legal assistant to continue in Arabic, however, he could not continue the conversation due to an emotional outburst, as expected at the other end. We realized that any further talk on the phone was not possible at that time, so we decided to drop the call. A follow-up call was made after about two hours by our legal assistant, who shared the details about the accident, the actions taken, and the plans for the repatriation of the remains. We also arranged for necessary assistance required for smooth handling over at the destination airport through the agency and the airline moving the cargo.

The next step was to monitor the progress of the

movement. The estimated total time for the flight was about twelve hours from start to end. Our travel desk was assigned the task to monitor the progress and sharing updates. After many hours of suspense and stress the team, finally had a sigh of relief when the flight took off from Dubai to Addis Ababa at around 9 P.M. Follow-up actions such as coordination at the destination, closure of legal aspects related to the case, and release of financial compensation to the next of kin were initiated and completed on the following days.

This situation was incredibly unique for various reasons. Firstly, there was no precedent- this underlines the statement repeated in this book at multiple places, that each crisis is unique. Secondly, it was of high sensitivity nature due to the unfortunate death, and the stature of a very senior person who was affected by the same. The situation was required to be handled with speed, accuracy, sensitivity, compassion, and calm. Under normal circumstances, it would have been my manager who would have taken the lead as the head of the department; however, his absence thrust this extremely challenging responsibility upon me.

The entire team was applauded by the leadership for the deft and swift handling of the situation with the required care and sensitivity.

As I reflect on the sequence of events, the key aspects that helped develop positive dynamics within this team (albeit small) that was created at the spur of the moment to manage this specific crisis are:

1. **Leader Needs to Recognize their Limitations:** As the leader called upon to manage this situation, I had

serious apprehensions that whether I would be able to handle the task due to the perceived lack of support owing to various contributing factors as highlighted in the description of the incident. However, I realized soon enough that without the assistance of subject matter experts such as the PRO and the legal assistant who was better equipped with language proficiency and familiarity with the government processes, I could not have managed this situation. They responded positively when I requested their immediate support.

2. **Ability to influence is critical in a crisis:** In a crisis, there could be a need to co-opt the participation of various stakeholders, even outside one's normal circle of influence. The ability to make the other stakeholders see the criticality of the requirements is imperative to draw their positive and quick alignment. Not only the leader but all the members of a crisis management team must have this ability to influence positive collaboration. The instances of coordination with the police, a diplomatic mission situated in a different country, and the airlines in this narration are examples.

3. **Acknowledging & leveraging the skills and capabilities of team members:** Knowing the capabilities within the team is essential in crisis leadership roles. This facilitates placing the right man for the right job. Examples are leveraging the expertise of the PRO and the legal assistant to coordinate with various external stakeholders such as the hospital authorities, Police, diplomatic mission and the airline. The team members felt motivated as

they were allowed to demonstrate the importance of their skills.

4. **Trust and respect foster positive dynamics:** Mutual trust within the team is the key differentiator in any crisis. Even in this narrated situation with various constraints as highlighted, a sense of trust was achieved through mutual respect as we went about doing various activities. The PRO and the legal assistant were not reporting to me directly in the normal course of work and thus I wasn't fully exposed to their capabilities. However, they were entrusted with important tasks and allowed the freedom to work in the same direction, which created a sense of respect and mutual trust quickly.

CASE 2: A DELUGE CANNOT DILUTE TEAM SPIRIT

The city of Mumbai was inundated by torrential rains on July 26, 2005. It was stated to be one of the highest-ever rainfalls in twenty-four hours, never received in over a century. The city suffered colossal devastation, with the loss of many lives and properties, and a significant negative impact on the economy.

I returned to India from the Middle East assignment in 2002 and was working with a reputed IT company in Mumbai as the functional head for all the support services. I was based out of the company HQ in Andheri.

On this fateful day, my organization had planned a press briefing on the new business strategy and product release. The event was scheduled from 3:30 to 5:30 P.M. at our development centre located in Navi Mumbai. Invitees included thirty senior journalists from various reputed media houses. The meeting was to be presided over by the Chairman of our Board of Directors along with other senior executive and directors. The participants started arriving at the development centre around 2 P.M.

The month of July is the peak of the monsoon season in the western region of the country and Mumbai always bears the brunt. So, when it started raining at around 1:30 P.M., it was like any other day in July for the people of Mumbai.

Planning to reach the Navi Mumbai development centre in about an hour, I started from Andheri at 1:30 P.M. The rains started intensifying after about fifteen to thirty minutes, and the entire sky turned dark. Traffic was a lot slower than usual. My driver was not able to see clearly through the heavy rain, and the waterlogged roads made progress extremely slow. The going was getting tougher and longer.

The main access road to our development centre was completely inundated, with many vehicles stuck on the flooded road. Fortunately, my driver knew an alternate route through residential areas, and we decided to take the detour. The inner roads, though flooded, had much lower water levels but were full of potholes, with many live electric wires blown down by heavy winds. After a nerve-racking drive, we finally reached the development centre at around 4:15 P.M.

I entered and saw a group of employees insisting with the administration staff to send them home on company buses. I updated the administration manager about the flood situation outside, which posed a huge safety risk. He told me that three buses had already been dispatched with about eighty employees. He added there are about one thousand people, including employees, customers, vendors, and visitors, currently in the building. By then, the rains had intensified, and the water level within the complex started rising. I met the Chairman and the head of HR and updated them on the situation outside and the potential risks for anyone moving out.

The journalists who had come for the press briefing were restless and insisted on being sent back to Mumbai in our buses. It was becoming difficult for the administration to manage to convince them. At this point, I went to the security control room and picked up the microphone of the emergency announcement system. After giving a brief account of the situation outside and the potential safety risks, I announced that we would neither send the buses nor allow anyone to step out. I explained that we would be a lot safer indoors than on the road. Everyone was advised to call up their families and inform them about their well-being and that they would be staying back in the office for the night.

We also told the administration manager at our Andheri office to make the same announcement. Luckily, the number of people in the Andheri office was far less.

This was easily done—but we soon realized the enormity of the problem facing us. There was no idea when the rains would stop. The biggest question was how we would accommodate nine hundred people in the office, for how long, and how we would arrange for their food and other necessities.

We got into a quick huddle to assess the situation and the options. The first and immediate requirement was to arrange food. The office cafeteria had only a few items and not enough raw materials to cater for one thousand people. A quick check revealed that all the food stalls in the complex were either closed or had run out of stock.

Our administration manager suggested we send out a task force on a couple of motorcycles to the nearest market to pick up whatever was available. This was a good idea but risky because of the flood situation outside. The question was also how much two people could carry on a bike if at all they were able to safely travel and find something in the market.

Under the circumstances, with no other option emerging, we decided to give it a try. Four of the admin staff and security team promptly volunteered. They went to the market on two motorcycles. The moments that followed were highly tense, as we were concerned about their safety.

After about thirty minutes, one of the task force members called to say that two buses that had been sent out earlier were stuck in floods with all the employees inside them. The focus of the mission immediately shifted to ensuring their safety. Turning the buses back was not possible due to the huge line of vehicles stranded on both sides. The only possible solution was to check for safe shelter in the nearby buildings and move the employees there. The task force took the initiative to find a few safe places, and the employees were evacuated.

This brought up another question: Where was the third bus? The task force could not locate it nearby. Finally, they were told to continue with their main task of sourcing supplies and returning to the safety of the office as quickly as possible. We were worried about losing contact with them, as the mobile network had begun faltering.

The task force managed to locate a shop and procured a few cartons of bread, chips, and biscuits, which they lugged on their backs and the sides of the bikes. They returned by about 8 P.M.

By then, the main power lines had been disconnected as a safety precaution by the authorities. We had to switch on the standby power generators but there was fuel for only ten hours of continuous operation, as per the standard business continuity protocols. That meant that if the main power was not restored soon, the generators would run out of fuel. An uninterrupted power supply was essential for the data centre and other critical infrastructure. The internet was the lifeline at this time, and we had to ensure it continued to be available.

After a quick analysis of the problem and options, we decided to reduce the power consumption in the five-storied building by bringing people together to fewer work floors and meeting rooms and switching off as many lights and power circuits as possible. Everyone cooperated and implemented these decisions. We also decided to run the generator for one hour at a time and rest it for thirty minutes.

By now most mobile connectivity was down—the saving grace was that the main telephone landline was still working, and the internet was also live. Messages from our employees deployed outside the country at client sites started pouring in, asking for help to check the welfare of their parents and relatives in various parts of the city. They were scared after watching media reports on the calamity.

The next critical requirement was to address the emails and calls reaching the front office from our associates abroad. We set up a control room in the front office itself and started logging the details of employees calling in. In parallel, efforts continued to find the whereabouts of the bus that was missing. The volume of calls and emails in the control room was extremely high. Many employees volunteered to support the effort, including our chairman, directors, and other senior leaders—this was leading from the front and was so inspiring. We formed more taskforces with specific assignments, such as providing support to the people on different floors, logging details from calls and emails, attending to the efforts of preventing the floodwaters from entering the building, fixing water leakages from the facade and other places in the building, etcetera. It was amazing to see all rising to the challenge and contributing their best.

Our chairman personally ensured that the journalists, who were our guests, ladies in the family way, and others needing special care were put up in the board room and cabins, and continuously supported for any need.

By about 11 P.M., the rains subsided, but water levels across the city remained high. By midnight, it became evident that we could not continue to run the generator set, as it had begun heating up. We quickly informed everyone and shut down the generator; the only lights now available were the emergency units in the building and torches with the security team.

The rest of the night was extremely challenging. The task forces continued to focus on their responsibilities. I, along with the head of HR, reviewed the emails and messages that were pouring in from our associates outside India. Many of them wanted us to reach out to their kin immediately and check on their welfare. We had great difficulty in explaining the overall situation, disruption of communication channels, and unsafe road conditions that rendered it impossible to go anywhere or get updates. We assured them that it would be our priority and that we would make all efforts under the challenging circumstances. A team of volunteers took up this task of coordination. The next morning a task force was commissioned to check on the welfare of the parents of some of our colleagues who were in deep distress.

As day broke on July 27, a frenzy of activities—including restoration of power, procuring additional diesel for the DG set, removing water seepage from the building, and organizing food for the stranded employees—kicked off. It was amazing that despite the challenges of the previous day and night, the team members were highly motivated and continued to make all the efforts needed.

The overall situation was normalized by about noon on July 27, with the partial operation of public transport. We decided to dispatch company buses to their usual destinations across the city. A team continued to track their progress to ensure that all employees reached their homes safely. The bus that had gone missing the previous day was also traced near a railway station, where it had got stuck in the floods; all employees in it had been able to take shelter in the station building and took trains to reach their homes when the services were restored. We set up a task force to connect with them and check on their welfare.

By the end of the day, we had completed all tasks;

fortunately, all our employees were safe, except a few who had fallen sick due to exposure to rain and floodwater. There was a lot of damage to the power station and other ancillaries in the basement of the building. The support teams continued to work on restoring operations.

A reflection of the chronology of events highlights the fact that our decision not to send people from the building was crucial in ensuring their safety. As the situation evolved, quick decisions and actions by the task forces—such as organizing food, shifting employees stranded on the road to nearby buildings, managing the power supply situation efficiently, handling anxious queries of employees outside India, etcetera—enabled us to manage the crisis successfully. These may appear to be small tasks, but when nearly one thousand people are stranded in one building in extremely unsafe surroundings, the perspective changes.

The significant enabler of this effective management of this crisis was the way the team understood the challenges and responded to the same with resolute focus.

Other factors such as communication and speed of action and decisions, like any other crisis, stand out from this experience.

Some of the key learnings over and above those mentioned earlier are as follows:

1. **Situational leadership is critical in crisis:** In an unprecedented crisis, when anxieties and confusion are at their peak, someone will be needed to take charge and guide the rest of the people. The confidence resolution and the ability to drive

positivity in the minds of impacted people are key differentiators. This leadership behaviour will drive others in the situation to step up and join hands to tide over the crisis. The action to convey the decision that no one would be allowed to move out of the building is an example.

2. **Thinking on the go enables quicker response:** In an unprecedented situation, one needs to think and find solutions for every problem that arises as the situation unravels. There will be the need to respond immediately, yet the decision needs to be based on a quick analysis of the situation and the potential future impact. The action by the team to explore supply availability by venturing out on bikes and later to check out on the employees' parents are shining examples of such quick thinking.

3. **A crisis can bring out the best in people:** Many individuals, including service providers, visitors, and senior leaders, irrespective of their personal or professional stature, stepped up and contributed their best to the overall efforts. Everyone stranded in the building accepted the realities and heeded the guidance of the task force. They helped each other to stay calm under these extremely difficult circumstances.

4. **Collaboration is the key:** Organizations with a strong culture of collaboration combined with the act of leading from the front by senior leaders spur positivity and motivation. Teams can produce wonders in a collaborative environment with flexibility and freedom to think, act, and contribute.

5. **Prudence in Resources management:** In any crisis where it is not clear how long the situation will last; it is important to ensure that resources are utilized wisely. Keep a close watch on critical resources and replenish them as quickly as possible.

6

Team Dynamics in Crisis – Summary

In this treatise, I have reflected on various aspects of leadership and team dynamics from an array of diverse and challenging situations or lived experiences from my professional life. Each of these narrated situations is unique in terms of the very nature of the crisis, the circumstances under which these had to be managed and the diverse composition of teams who were part of the crisis management.

There could be numerous factors that influence the outcomes of a crisis. My focus here has been to explore the interplay between the situation, the crisis leader and the team members that create a positive behavioural and functional relation during the process, leading to the desired outcomes.

I have had opportunities to lead teams in diverse environments such as the regular army, a commando unit, and the corporate environments at country and global levels. Experience in developing a well-knit, cohesive, and dynamic team was always the foremost requirement and the most challenging task in these diverse environments.

Building and leading a team could be comparatively easy in the army, as the organization has a stable structure with well-defined leadership roles and team composition. The team members are trained together and they live together, thus leading to stronger bonding and trust among the people in the teams.

On the contrary, building a cohesive team in a corporate organization is a far more challenging task. This is essentially due to the dynamic nature of the corporate organizational structure. Changes are frequent in the corporate organization structure due to varying factors such as re-aligned business models, market dynamics, frequent employee churn and multitude of other factors as could be occurring in the overall business ecosystems. Diverse backgrounds and mindsets of people in a corporate add another dimension to the complexity of building cohesive teams in corporates. There is a tendency to work in silos focusing only on one's defined job role and key result areas. For anything new to be done, the foremost question would be "what is in it for me". The distributed model of operation wherein various parts of the organization work from different locations further exacerbates the leadership challenge of team building.

A strong and cohesive team and positive team dynamics are not built by people just working under one roof. It is a deliberate process where people trust, appreciate, respect, enable, and are concerned for each other. Corporate leaders are required to build and nurture this environment and culture in the organizations, however large or small they are. The leader needs to know the team members more than just a person at work, understand the strengths and opportunities for development for each one of them, help the person see the purpose of the job role in a larger spectrum and appreciate the value created by what he or she does, irrespective the job cluster, designation or position. The leader needs to create and foster a learning culture to continually enhance team capabilities.

Providing opportunities where the team members can leverage their capabilities to the best to achieve desired results and applauding such success works wonders in creating a cohesive and energized team. The leader needs to be seen as one among the team and not someone on a different pedestal- this is most critical when things go wrong. The leadership motto must be "when my team wins, it is them, and when they do not, it is me".

In a crisis, diverse teams come together as a Task Force or Cross-functional Team to deal with the problem and ensure the least impact on the organization. The outcome would largely depend on how the teams collaborate and converge their efforts and energies to manage the situation. Developing positive team dynamics in the shortest available time is a critical challenge for the crisis leader. Some of the important aspects that would contribute towards developing positive team dynamics are summarized below:

1. **Purpose-Driven Teams Engage Positively:** It is important to highlight the purpose for which the crisis management task force has been constituted. The team members need to be aware of the enterprise risk being managed through the task force crisis and the trust that is reposed on their ability to deal with

the same. Reiterate the criticality of the task at hand and how their actions would translate to delivering a positive outcome for the organization. A clearly defined purpose will drive the group to act as a cohesive team and perform beyond the functional boundaries.

2. **Define Specific objectives and empower ownership at individual/small group levels:** The crisis response would need an array of activities to be undertaken simultaneously. Individuals and smaller teams need to be empowered to own these and take actions as appropriate.

3. **Break the silos:** The task force or CFT needs to believe, behave and act as one cohesive unit. Functional boundaries must be erased and collective focus should be brought on the immediate tasks and objectives.

4. **Provide the framework and guidelines:** Even with a well-documented and rehearsed crisis response procedure, it is possible that all the members of the task force are not aware of the same. It is important to ensure that all members are familiarized with the framework.

5. **Provide the wherewithal and logistics:** The crisis manager and the teams need to stay calm, peaceful, and Confident as they deal with the situation and this cannot be possible if they are deprived of basic needs.

SPACE FOR READER'S REFLECTIONS

....
....
....
....
....
....
....
....
....
....
....
....
....
....
....
....
....
....
....
....

SECTION 3

Resilience in Crisis Management

I can be changed by what happens to me
But I refuse to be reduced by it

—**Maya Angelou**

7

Resilience – The Key Differentiator in Crisis

Crises and challenges are an inescapable part of our professional and personal lives.

Resilience is broadly defined as the ability to absorb and withstand crises and challenges, influence changes and build inner robustness from these experiences. Organizational resilience is the ability to anticipate, respond and adapt to changes that can occur due to unexpected disruptions.

Resilience does not get created by default. It is indeed established by a deliberate design. There are innate capabilities in individuals and organizations, however, it requires efforts and actions to nurture these to spring out in the hour of need and sustain it over a long period in the face of continual adversities.

There are many theories and models on building resilience at the organizational level encompassing various elements such as products, services, processes, technology, people and culture. Developing resilience involves building adaptability, diversity, modularity, redundancy, and contingency plans and integrating the same into the overall operational ecosystem, internally and externally.

All these theoretical aspects are put to acid test in a destructive crisis scenario. Every practical crisis brings in new insights and learning that need to be embedded into all the components of resilience design as a continual improvement. This will truly bolster the capability to withstand a destructive crisis, restore the original state and continue with business as usual – and therefore ensure organizational resilience which is essential for organizational survival.

The focus is this book is on the resilience of people at the individual level and how it can play up at the collective level in a crisis.

Organizations are made of people of different make and mould. People act and react diffculty in every crisis scenario. Resilience at a personal level plays up first in a crisis and it can significantly influence the collective resilience of people in the larger organization. Therefore the foundation for building organizational resilience is at the individual level.

At the individual level, resiliency is a basic human instinct based on thoughts, behaviours, and actions. However, unless these characteristics are harnessed and reinforced a collective, positive response as expected in the face of a destructive situation cannot be guaranteed. Therefore, the primary focus while building organizational resilience should be on how to embolden these characteristics in people, which make them resilient at the personal level and resultantly at the collective level the organization tends to be resilient.

Learning from lived experiences validates the theories about the essential enablers of resilience at the personal level. These are confidence, optimism, tolerance, persistence, ability to deal with ambiguity and most importantly thinking beyond self. An organization with a culture that nurtures and fosters these individual traits is likely to develop a pool of resilient people and thus would find emboldened actions originating from the positive mindset of people in the face of a crisis.

An organization with resilient people enabled and emboldened with a robust framework of processes and led by resolute leadership is better prepared to manage a crisis.

8

Case References – Resilience in Crisis

CASE 1: PROLONGED COVID-19 PANDEMIC – GRIT AND RESILIENCE ENDURES PERSISTING PERIL

The uncertainty and ambiguity around the COVID-19 pandemic continued for a prolonged period of two years at unimaginable and unmanageable magnitude. The initial response by countries was to impose lockdowns and restrictions on everyday activities, in a bid to contain the spread while the experts grappled with this unprecedented development to devise the right mechanism to deal with the same. Despite these measures, the disease spread like wildfire across the continents debilitating every aspect of human life. It took more than six months since the first reported cases in Wuhan, China, for healthcare experts to conclude the nature of the virus and its mode of transmission. Initially, there were differing views about the transmission–whether airborne or through surface contact. After weeks of debate within the expert community, it was finally concluded by the WHO that the main mode of transmission is through the air. Based on this confirmation, the basic guidelines for prevention termed "COVID-Appropriate Behaviour" (CAB) were defined and implemented by governments in a bid to reduce transmission. However, the most critical need of the hour was the speedy development of vaccines. The rapid development of a vaccine is not a small feat—history bears evidence that the normal process to develop a vaccine takes 10 to 15 years to get completed. The fact that scientists have been studying and researching various forms of coronaviruses for over 50 years and the advancement of technology enabling faster process cycles contributed much towards accelerating the development of vaccines.

The COVID virus, however, turned out to be smarter than expected as it continued to mutate and with each mutation, its virulence and impact kept increasing. The typical cycle of infection was different from the initial Alpha to the latest Omicron variants. It was now clear that this pandemic was not going to end soon. Indomitable human hope and spirits continued to be high even in these circumstances with news about progress in vaccine development trickling in.

In response to this situation, multiple stakeholders displayed unprecedented collaboration and speed of action to enable the pharmaceutical industry to develop and evaluate vaccines for COVID-19. This, aided by the advancement in technology accelerated the process of developing, and testing in the laboratories followed by successful clinical trials resulting in many vaccines. These vaccines were approved by the WHO within months as opposed to decades in the past.

Vaccination of the entire population was an onerous task—governments adopted a staggered approach and by the end of 2020, vaccination drives were well underway in many countries. As the vaccination coverage progressed, economic activities resumed at varying times in different countries, albeit in a controlled manner.

The prolonged pandemic had enforced what is now called a "new normal" on human life, which meant accepting a restricted style of day-to-day life and work. Organizations across the globe initially made bold announcements about resuming business as usual; however, the dynamic nature of COVID infections forced abandonment of all such plans. Business operations continued to be in the remote work model. By March 2021, after a year of remote and business continuity mode of operations, organizations reconciled to the fact that this situation is here to stay. New concepts and theories on the future of work kept experts and consultants busy. Many governments started declaring their victory over the pandemic. This sense of relief was short-lived as the situation took an unprecedented and ugly turn with the onslaught of a new variant of the COVID virus named "Delta". Wave-2 raged across continents for over three months, with the number of cases soaring to three times that of Wave-1. The healthcare infrastructure collapsed in many countries, especially in India, resulting in the loss of many lives, delivering a severe cascading impact on the economy and the psyche of people.

Businesses continued to maintain human safety as paramount amidst these challenges and this was a truly appreciable fact. However, managing the fine balance between employee safety and business continuity in such a fast-changing dynamic situation for a prolonged period has been extremely challenging. The situation turned out to be more complex with many other crises emerging during this period when the personal capacity of people, especially managers, was stretched beyond limits. While the mode of remote work was easier in many ways for organizations and employees, its prolonged persistence had various negative impacts. Decline in collaboration within teams, the ability to kindle innovative ideas and sustaining organizational culture became major concerns for the organizations. This was aggravated by a steep increase in attrition translating to the need for hiring new resources. These new employees were faced with the unique situation of being virtually inducted and collaborating with people whom they had never met in person. On the other hand, employees experienced weariness resulting from the monotonous nature of the new normal. People had moved away from large city locations from where they worked before the onset of COVID to smaller towns and villages in remote areas. A sizable percentage of these employees faced a productivity impact as they were not able to engage with colleagues in focused discussions on critical business requirements, diminishing borders between work and personal timings, infrastructure limitations such as power and broadband outages as well as a lack of privacy in the home environment. Added to this was the news of colleagues and family members being infected by COVID with succumbing to it.

The sum of these circumstances was the impact on the psychological well-being of people. The ability to sustain this needed tremendous mental strength–or, in other words, Resilience. How did people endure this challenge for so long?

What impact would this prolonged constrained living and working situation have on work styles and attitudes and, more importantly, how did they deal with this at their level and managed to address the crises on both personal and professional fronts?

In this section, I will try to explore the aspects of team play, leadership and resilience under these unprecedented circumstances of prolonged crisis, with real-life incidents wherein individuals and teams, demonstrated outstanding dedication to respond to situations, espousing individual and organizational resilience.

The first of these occurred in August 2020 at a facility that housed business-critical technical equipment supporting global business. This facility in effect is the technical nerve centre and is listed as a vital installation of national importance. Any act of omission or commission that could incapacitate it is bound to have a cascading impact rendering many customer businesses unviable. This could lead to significant business impact, both in terms of revenue losses and reputational damage for the organization. It is therefore natural that such a facility is operationally managed and maintained with the highest priority. It was in this facility that a major power outage occurred on that day. What seemed to be a routine maintenance activity turned out to be a major business management crisis. The reasons for these multiple failures were of course identified through a deliberate and detailed root cause analysis post-incident. As is the case in managing such disasters, my focus here would be on how the team responded to the situation and reinstated the operations with minimum impact on business.

It was around 10 P.M. when I got a call from the business head informing me about the major power outage at this critical facility that was affecting our business globally. The business head was receiving a steady flow of customer escalation calls about the cascading impact on their businesses. This situation was intriguing as there are multiple backups and redundancies for uninterrupted power supply, which includes battery banks and diesel generators. These backup systems should have run automatically within a few seconds of a failure in the main power grid. Immediately after the call from the business head, I spoke to the head of engineering who shared the disturbing news that all backup systems had indeed failed. The need of the hour was to make power available without any further loss of time—as each minute of delay would translate to millions of dollars of adverse impact on business and, of course, the organization's reputation of being the most dependable business partner. An immediate huddle with the team proved that the UPS (equipment ensuring Uninterrupted Power Supply), which is the first level of redundancy, failed and the DG (diesel generator), which is the second level and should have auto-started in such a scenario also did not work. While the grid power was restored in about 15 minutes, the main power panels, gadgets, and circuitry had burnt out, making them unusable.

The task at hand appeared intimidating at that late hour and in an environment with so many controls and restrictions on activities due to COVID. The moral of the operations team was at the lowest ebb as their credibility was at stake. The sequence of actions thereafter was a true testimonial of situational leadership. The site engineering head at once took up the lead. Assembling his team, he quickly reviewed the situation and took an on-the-spot decision to get the power circuit charged without any further loss of time. He spoke to a neighbouring organization and persuaded them to allow the use of their generator. This required additional power lines to be connected with the neighbours' DG set. The team worked on a war footing to set up the connection and power was restored in about 45 minutes. However, this was a temporary solution as the DG set could support only for about six hours and the main power had to be reconnected, battery bank failure was investigated and rectified, and our own DG set was repaired before it conked out. Overall, it was mission impossible.

What we saw thereafter was a team of four, which included third-party contractors, taking on this enormous task nonchalantly, and moving the mountains to restore business continuity and consequently customer confidence, within a few hours. The head of engineering voluntarily went to the site by road overcoming many travel restrictions imposed due to the COVID pandemic. The team collectively mobilized all resources including transporting new batteries required for the battery bank from another city and exhorting external stakeholders to step up and ease the restoration of power without delay. While doing this, the team leader had to take many decisions beyond his regular remit. In the entire process of managing the situation, the team displayed resolute determination and went beyond the normal call of duty to deal with the crisis and resolve it. There were many factors and conditions, both external and internal, which could have rendered the situation beyond their control. What prompted them to do this? As revealed by the team during the debrief, the realization that their professional competence and credibility were at stake propelled them to do what they did. They also highlighted the trust they had in support from senior management and this emboldened their decisions on the ground. On the question of ignoring their safety, the univocal answer was they would have done anything for the sake of saving their professional credibility. This kind of commitment and ownership can only be experienced in a corporate environment where teams have complete trust and confidence in their leaders and is an excellent example of resilience at the individual and team levels.

The second situation involved the safe evacuation of our employees from Myanmar. The country had undergone a military coup during which the elected government was overthrown. The law-and-order situation in the country was worsening day-by-day with demonstrations by people opposing the new regime, and control measures by the military leading to clashes and arson increasing day-by-day, endangering the safety of people. To make the situation worse, mobile communications and the internet were shut down.

We had more than twenty employees and families from India based at a client site near the capital city of Myanmar. While the client assured us of all safety measures initially, it became clear as the days went by that the situation was fast deteriorating and there was nothing much the client could do to ensure the safety of our employees. This led to concerted efforts to persuade the client to allow their repatriation. After securing this permission, the subsequent challenge was to arrange their safe evacuation – first from their residences to the airport about thirty kilometres away and then find a suitable flight to bring them back safely to India. The global mobility support team sprang into action here and after extraordinary efforts of talking to the diplomatic mission and airlines, it was finally possible to arrange the necessary tickets. This action was followed by close monitoring of the movement of the employees – the risk was further compounded by the military not allowing people to move. This permission was secured by the team with great difficulty and the group of employees and families were transported to the airport in special vehicles. Thereafter, their flight was coordinated, and they arrived safely in India. Throughout this mission, the team demonstrated complete ownership and accountability to make sure every aspect of the evacuation was coordinated seamlessly. This was a task where the probability of a positive outcome was bleak. The team was fully aware of this; however, that did not deter them and throughout the operation, they demonstrated great ownership and personal responsibility towards making the evacuation successful. In the debrief discussions, it became evident again that the team was driven by professional commitment and a sense of empathy towards their colleagues in distress.

The third case study is a shining example of teams going beyond the normal call of duty even at the cost of their inconvenience. As the situation was seeming to become the "new normal", the pandemic manifested differently this time with a new variant of the virus called "Delta", starting in April 2020. This variant had a much faster infection rate and was more lethal. Many countries came under its super-spreading grip within weeks of it being identified and yet again we were caught unprepared. The number of cases requiring hospitalization shot up rapidly and the medical fraternity was perplexed to see that the previously tested treatment methods were not effective against this new virus variant. Within a matter of days, there was a severe shortage of COVID testing kits in the market, which led to delays in determining infections leading to a cascading impact of more infections and serious conditions of the infected. Besides, the scarcity of ambulances and the non-availability of hospital beds added to the shortage of essential medicines. This unprecedented development threw all systems out of gear – with the number of infected persons and deaths mounting day-by-day, all hope and positivity that emerged after the vaccinations, came crashing down. Wave-2, as it was called, was ominous.

India was one of the countries worst hit by Wave-2. My organization had the largest employee base across cities in India – which meant increased risk for them. We were shocked to see the rapid increase in the number of employees getting infected in a quick time. The situation was turning into a crisis within a crisis. We promptly realized the need for a different method to tackle this new development. A separate task force was formed immediately to respond to this new challenge. A help desk was set up with the charter to extend round-the-clock support to employees and families. The help desk worked continuously to support the requirements of ambulances, hospital admissions, and sourcing of essential medicines that poured in at odd hours. The biggest challenge the team faced was to manage their on-presence of mind and composure and stay calm while handling the desperate calls for support to save someone's life. This is when many of the task force members had their family members impacted—it takes a tremendous amount of willpower to deal with such a situation. The brutal second wave of COVID prevailed for over two months, playing havoc with the lives of people across the country; it had the same impact on our employee population too. Many a time, when we received requests for help, we knew there was nothing we could do to help and that was a devastating feeling. It was amazing to see how the team, who did not have the professional training to deal with such situations, truly rose to the occasion. Despite the constraints and challenges, the team ensured round-the-clock availability and mobilized resources by reaching out to various sources including personal contacts.

The fourth incident that occurred during this challenging period was the evacuation of an employee and family who were stranded in a heavily flooded interior location. The month of July 2021 witnessed heavy rains in the western part of India. This employee was working remotely from his native village – as was allowed during the BCM mode of operations. On that day, his village was completely flooded because of the torrential rains. Water had entered the house and the level was rising fast. The family was in shock and distress. Around midnight, when they found no help coming to their rescue, the employee used our emergency support contact number to raise the alarm as a last resort. The team at the emergency response centre was managing regular calls for support related to COVID and this kind of call was a total surprise. They were not prepared to tackle a requirement like this. They immediately alerted the security and safety team who, after assessing the situation, knew that there was nothing much they could do as the location was far away in a remote area. They contacted the government disaster management authorities; however, they were not in a position to respond immediately as they were already overwhelmed by the number of cases.

The team was cognizant of the increasing risk to life with every passing minute and the possible consequences if immediate support is not extended to the colleague in distress. In a quick huddle with the team leader, they evaluated the situation, possible response actions and the wherewithal required to provide any support. The team realized the hard fact that we did not have the resources to initiate a rescue mission. The decision, therefore, was to contact another organization in the neighbourhood, that had the reach and resources to extend support in the marooned remote area. However, it was not sure whether they will be able to mobilize resources to support this particular requirement, as they would be committed in other locations. To the utter delight of our team, this organization obliged and immediately mobilized its disaster response team. This team travelled over sixty kilometres at night braving torrential rains and bad roads to reach the marooned area. They were constantly in touch with the distressed employee. On reaching the area, they set out for the exact location where the family was marooned using Gemini boats and evacuated the family to safety. This was an act of commitment beyond imagination. Here again, the question is what prompted the team from a different organization to respond positively in such a high-risk situation. The amazing response from their team leader and members was that they had done what they considered their duty and if they were in such a situation, they would have expected others too to respond likewise.

What stands out from all these real-life cases is that a well-motivated and led team can assume responsibility to spring to action under any challenging situation. The basic human instinct of empathy and ownership will emerge when teams believe in their professional capability augmented by the psychological safety that they are not alone in the battle. The psychological safety aspect emerges from the trust and belief among the team members and their confidence in the assured support from leadership. This kindles a sense of empowerment to take critical decisions on the ground to respond positively to challenging situations. This assumes significant importance in a corporate environment.

Determination and endurance are the most important human behaviours that are tested in any prolonged state of crisis. These are indeed the bedrock of resilient characteristics in people. The outcome of any crisis would depend on how these inherent characteristics are manifested at individual and collective levels during a crisis. Developing and sustaining these behavioural aspects is the key challenge for leaders dealing with crises in a corporate environment.

The crises narrated here reiterate the critical role that resilience at individual levels plays towards emboldening organizational resilience.

This case study and the specific situations discussed within this, bring out many crisis management lessons on leadership, team dynamics and resilience.

1. **Organizational culture of enabling and facilitating leadership fosters resilience:** This helps to build a positive mindset, compassion and a sense of confidence which play a crucial role in developing

individual resilience. Enabling entails providing all the resources, wherewithal, training, and guidance as appropriate from time to time and building a sense of empowerment and confidence in the team. Facilitating would mean being with the team through word and action and creating an environment of positivity and optimism while dealing with adversities.

2. **The Duty of Care nurtures Emotional Resilience:** The pandemonium caused by the Delta variant of Covid was massive and it had a deep impact on the mental well-being of the employees. Leaders had to demonstrate utmost care in handling delicate emotional situations. The leaders' task was extremely difficult when team members reached out for support for themselves or family members, and it was not possible to mobilize any resources or extend support. However, the ability to empathize, stay positive and continue to provide the confidence that we are together in this, had a positive impact on the psychological well-being of people, which helped them to be strong and resilient.

3. **Flexibility of thought and actions:** The leader's role demands the ability to bring out the best in the teams. As a leader, one would have to deal with multiple challenges at the same time. The leader would need to stay undeterred and demonstrate a strong belief in the team's ability, the flexibility of mind to accept and deal with situations as they unfold and the ability to take quick decisions, which will influence and bolster the team's behaviour translating to positive outcomes in a crisis. During the peak of the Delta

variant impact, leaders faced the challenge of the need to ensure the continuity of many business-critical functions and operations at the required levels even with depleted staff availability. This could not have been achieved without the ability to modify certain operational procedures which could then be managed with reduced hands on the job or even with staff members who were not well trained. Leaders were required to continuously be "on the job" with these teams. Those leaders who could not adapt to this changed environment found themselves at a loss in these situations.

4. **Crisis Communication:** As in any crisis, the significance of timely and clear communication was found to be that of the key differentiator. In any situation where there is chaos all around what keeps people engaged and optimistic is how they receive information which is reliable and timely. The challenge of ensuring this information flow in a scenario where people are scattered across locations is even more complicated. Leaders would be required to personally connect with the team members, over and above the routine e-mail communications. This is an added responsibility that all leaders must shoulder willingly.

5. **Resourcefulness:** The ability to identify and Leverage capabilities outside one's immediate circle of influence. Many a time it would so happen that one does not have all the resources and wherewithal to deal with the emergent crisis. The leader would be called upon to look for resources and support beyond the limit of their organization. It Is Important

to recognize this limitation quickly and reach out to other organizations in the neighbourhood for support. If such collaboration requirement is assessed and built into the crisis management plans at the preparation stage itself, the process at the time of need becomes much easier and quicker.

CASE 2: EVERYTHING AROUND YOU MIGHT BE SINKING, BUT NOT YOUR RESOLVE

Torrential rains lashed Chennai and various other parts of Tamil Nadu in the last week of November 2015. As per official statements, this was the highest rainfall the city had received in over a century and had a devastating impact across the area. Most parts of the city and the suburbs were submerged in deep water, endangering lives. Even with technology and improved weather monitoring and forecasting systems, this intensity of the rains and the resultant mayhem was not foreseen, and as a result, there was no proactive response mechanism put in place. Continuous torrential rainfall for many days in the upper regions resulted in a large quantity of rainwater swamping the Adayar river, which flows through the city of Chennai, causing flooding along its course.

I was working with a large business conglomerate based in Mumbai with responsibilities that included the entire gamut of business support services. Chennai city had many of our business critical infrastructure, a large employee population and multiple office facilities spread across various locations in the city. The torrential rains caused significant disruption to our operations. We had established a security command centre to monitor the developing situation. As the rains continued, we were able to invoke business continuity plans and announce working from home for most employees before the situation worsened. A local task force was set up to continuously monitor the developments.

The havoc of torrential rains continued through the first week of December. On December 3, 2015, I was travelling from Mumbai to Pune for official work. As I was driving along the expressway, I received a call from one of our senior leaders based outside India. The person apprised me that he had received a frantic message from another senior colleague based in Chennai. The message mentioned the rapidly rising flood water levels near his house and that the safety of his family was at imminent risk and this could be his last message. The leader who called me mentioned that after receiving this message all attempts to contact this impacted person in Chennai failed. There was an urgent requirement to do something immediately, to ascertain the status and ensure his safety. I assured the senior person who called me that, we will take all possible actions immediately.

After finishing the call, I contacted a senior member of my team in Chennai (we will refer to him as G), who was also the nominated leader for business continuity and disaster recovery for this scenario. I shared the details of the concern received from the senior leader. G, like me, also had a defence background and we were quickly able to carry out an appreciation of the situation to assess what could be possibly done under the prevailing conditions. As per G's assessment, the location of the person in distress was one of the worst hit by heavy floods. Access roads to that area were completely submerged in deep waters. The only possible mode of travel to that place was by boat and this was under the control of the local government agencies pressed into action. G's efforts to connect with local authorities and seek their help proved futile. Time was running out, and something was required to be done quickly.

After some more discussions over mobile phones, we decided to allow the required time for G and the team to explore the best possible options. G called me back after about fifteen minutes and said, "I have discussed the task and the situation with the security manager. There is no other way to get any information about the person in distress but to go to the location and check out physically. We need to send a rescue mission" He updated that they have there are a few volunteers from the security service provider team who are good swimmers, and ready to move out immediately in their emergency support vehicle. He wanted my clearance to launch the mission.

This was an exceedingly difficult decision to make. Sitting away from the crisis location I was not fully aware of the actual situation on the ground and the level of risk involved in sending out such a mission. The safety of the team members who had volunteered to go to the distressed location in a boat was a serious concern. I asked G if he was certain that it was the best option and how safe it would be. He shared a quick plan that the team would drive to a location as close to the place of distress as they could, and then secure a boat to reach the exact location of the residence of the person in distress. He added that the team members were good swimmers and motivated to take on this task. G and I discussed the safety aspects, the need to continuously monitor the progress of the team and when a decision would need to be made to abandon the mission in the interest of personal safety. After many moments of deep thinking, I asked G and the team to go ahead with the rescue mission. Immediately after this, I informed my manager through a series of WhatsApp messages about the situation, the requirement of sending the rescue mission and how it is being launched.

All this was happening while I was on the road away from our office. I got a call back from G that they have launched a rescue team. Everything seemed to be going as per plan, however, the progress of the team was slow due to prevailing road conditions.

At this juncture, I decided to continue my journey to our Pune office and reach there as quickly as possible. G and I were in constant communication over the mobile phone. Due to weak mobile network patches along the Mumbai-Pune expressway, we lost mobile connectivity after some time. This led to heightened tension and stress levels. Connectivity was established after about forty-five minutes, and I called up G for a progress update. The condition of the roads hampered progress and the team had still not reached the location. They were a few kilometres away from the location of distress. Heavy flooding prevented any further movement by vehicle. G said that the team was trying to secure a boat locally. He also expressed his apprehensions about the rising water level and other safety risks that might hamper or prevent any further action if they were not able to secure a boat soon enough. There were no further updates from G for quite some time; an uneasy calm prevailed.

At around 5 P.M., he called up to say "Sir, mission accomplished. The team was able to get hold of a boat from another rescue mission in the area. They reached the location of the house and rescued the entire family of five who had taken shelter on the roof of the building". It was such a great relief to hear these words. The mission was extremely risky and the challenges were enormous. Even then the team went about it without caring for their safety. This was an incredibly brave feat for the team.

The news of this extraordinary rescue effort and its success under the most challenging circumstances was shared with my manager and other leaders immediately. We received numerous messages of appreciation.

After some time, my manager called to personally convey his appreciation. He was amazed by the action taken by the team but was also concerned that it was such a huge risk to take. He asked, "How did you guys even decide to take such a grave risk. Did you consider what would have been the consequences if something had gone wrong with the safety of this rescue team? ". My answer was that we had evaluated all options and under the circumstances, there were only two possibilities – either to send the rescue to the team or not to send it. The leader and his family who were in a distressed situation were probably at much higher risk. So the team decided that they will take this risk to ensure the safety of this colleague and the family. The team on the grounds had confidence that they could safely execute the mission and that they trusted in the support from the manager and leaders should the mission fail.

This event had a profound impact on the organization and its leaders. This was a significant morale booster for G, his team and me as a crisis manager and people leader.

127

The commitment and courage shown by the team, including the people from a third-party service provider, were unparalleled and unbelievable. The members of the rescue mission were from third-party service providers, and while all of them were swimmers, they did not have any specific training to carry out such a mission in heavy flood waters. The situation was that the entire city of Chennai and its suburbs were completely inundated and heavy rains were still pouring – their own families in different parts of the city would have been impacted in such a scenario. Even then, they did not worry and rose above and beyond the call of their regular duty at the peril of their safety to accomplish this incomparable feat.

It was the can-do attitude of G and the team that made all the difference in this extremely challenging and high-risk situation. This is a shining example of resilience at the personal and team level. As a recognition of this audacious action in the face of extreme challenges, the entire team was felicitated and awarded by the senior leadership. G was recognized with the highest internal award.

This case is a true testimonial of all the key ingredients for successful crisis management – viz, leadership, positive team dynamics and resilience. Some of the important lessons that can be learnt from this case are:

1. **Enormity of the task accentuates the sense of responsibility and aids in Resilience:** This is a true statement for both the leader and the team. The bigger the challenge, the more it spurs the sense of responsibility and stimulates the urge to respond to it in the best manner. Resilient people will face a challenging situation boldly and take it to face. The

team on the ground in this case example had the option to say, nothing can be done with the flood waters all around, no equipment and no trained person to operate in such a high-risk situation. However, they did not do so and chose to fight the crisis.

2. **Igniting the super capabilities of people stimulates positivity and resilience:** Crisis brings out the best behaviour and attitudes. True character is revealed in the way you react when faced with a daunting situation. The leader should have the ability to recognize the capabilities of the team members and ignite their morale, motivation, and self-esteem to raise their performance to the highest possible level. The security guards, despite not being trained to operate in flood waters, with good swimming and boat operating skills came forward to take on this high-risk mission. Their willingness to take up the challenge is the true embodiment of selflessness and dedication to duty which is a hallmark of resilience.

3. **Sense of trust accentuates resilient response in a crisis:** The bond that develops between the leader and team in an enabling and facilitating environment lays a strong foundation for Trust. It acts as the binding glue in a team. When the team members are confident that someone has their back, they will step up to deliver resilient and positive behaviour in crises.

4. **Freedom and flexibility of action at the point of contact are critical:** People who are present at the location of the crisis would have the exact pulse of the situation and are therefore best placed to evaluate the options to respond to the situation in the best

manner. It is imperative to give such people the freedom and flexibility to act in the best way to deal with the situation. In this case, G and the team had complete freedom and flexibility to initiate the best response action based on their judgement of the situation.

5. **Initiative and presence of mind accelerate crisis response:** Throughout the crisis, there were sterling examples of the initiative by the team, at leadership, individual, and collective levels. Marshalling the resources required and making the best use of them is the key to a positive outcome in a crisis. This aspect was well demonstrated by the task force managing the crisis. Using the emergency vehicle to launch the task force and after sourcing a boat from the local authorities to continue with the mission in such adverse situations are good examples of initiative and application of presence of mind.

CASE 3: CONCURRENT CRISES ARE RESILIENCE FORTIFIED

This incident is from my Army service days and occurred in October 1994, in an operational area along India's northern border, marked as the Line of Control (LoC).

I was back at my parent army unit after a tour of duty with the elite National Security Guards (Black Cat Commandos), the federal reserve special force of India. I had been promoted to the rank of Major upon returning to my unit. After completing the mandatory induction and operational familiarization, I was assigned the command of a group of troops (a company) along the LoC. After a few months, I was appointed adjutant and moved back to the HQ at the base location. In the LoC scenario, the unit HQ is situated at the base or rear location, while the rest of the troops are deployed at the front on the high ground along the LoC.

The fateful day of the incident narrated here unfolded like any other, with the routine operational tasks as occur in all army units. In the evening, the final match of the inter-company hockey tournament was scheduled at the base location. Sports and games are an integral part of army life. It serves to keep the troops and officers physically fit and mentally agile while bonding them into cohesive teams. Most importantly, sports ignite a competitive spirit, which is the foundation of any fighting unit. It is natural, therefore, to see army men engaged in competitive sports, irrespective of the location or operational environment they are in.

Being deployed on the LoC, all routine activities needed to be ended before dusk. Therefore, the hockey match was scheduled to end by 4:30 P.M. As the adjutant, I had issued necessary coordinating orders related to all the operational aspects and the sports competition. Everything went off as planned. The game was very well played between two highly competent teams, leading to a nail-biting finish. Officers and troops moved back to their respective posts and locations per operational procedures.

It was my daily routine to go back to the adjutant's office after the evening games sessions got over, to check the letters and documents received by mail (dak as it is termed in the army) and move them for further processing, which was an important function of the adjutant's role. On this particular day, after attending to the paperwork, at the office, I walked towards my accommodation in the officers' mess area. My residential room was located on elevated ground, and there were about forty steps to be climbed to reach the place. The unit telephone exchange, the lifeline provider in an operational area, was located halfway up the steps.

As I started climbing the steps, I could see the telephone exchange operator on duty, standing outside the exchange and waving his hands frantically towards me. I hurried up the steps to reach where he was, I was called into the exchange and a telephone handset was thrust into my hands immediately. I sensed that there was some urgency, it was usual in the operational area where we were deployed in. As I talked on the phone, I realized that there were two calls connected in parallel with the commanding officer (CO) of our unit, and the officer in charge of one of the operational units (a company) deployed along the LoC.

The CO, in his usual tone, said, "CT, we have a problem" and asked the officer to explain the details of the problem on hand. What I heard from the other officer was a piece of shocking news – he said that one of our vehicles carrying provisions to a forward post on the LoC has met with an accident and it is stuck in an area under direct observation of the troops deployed on the other side of the border and that they are firing their weapons aimed to the area of this stranded vehicle. Our troops were not able to reach the vehicle because of incessant heavy machine gun firing. It appeared that the driver and his buddy had been hit by the bullets and sustained injuries. I looked at my watch; it was almost 6 P.M., and daylight was fading. It was evident that if we did not initiate a recovery operation quickly, it could lead to further complications.

The CO took an immediate decision to o go to the incident site at the LoC and asked me and the second-in-command of the unit to coordinate the required support and logistics from the base location. As the adjutant, it was my responsibility to be the pivot to coordinate the operations with the troops on the ground and with the higher HQ. There was another young officer who had recently joined the unit at the base location and who could also be pressed into taking the required action. While the CO was getting into his vehicle to drive up to the incident location, we received confirmation about the driver of the stranded vehicle succumbed to his injuries at the accident site.

To put things in perspective, the situation that prevails along the LoC is termed that of "a-no-war-no-peace" and cross-border firing is common. However, an incident of this nature, in which a vehicle is incapacitated, and a soldier killed, was extremely serious. Such incidents attract the attention of everyone in the higher echelons of command in the army.

It was critical to take immediate action to recover the vehicle and the body of the killed soldier. The recovery operations commenced immediately, however, it was getting hampered due to ceaseless firing from the other side. Additional resources were mobilized and the tactics required to abate the firing from across were also initiated. The CO personally provided leadership and oversight for the entire operation in situ. Coordination of support requirements, continuous monitoring of developments, and periodic updates to the HQ were the responsibilities managed by the three of us at the base location.

Intense and difficult operations to recover the vehicle continued until well past midnight. I was completely engrossed in monitoring the progress minute by minute, through the field telephone. Around that time, I received a call from the medical inspection room (MI room) that one of the soldiers who had played in the hockey match the previous evening had been brought into the medical room with complaints of uneasiness. I checked the basic details about the person and recognized that he was one of our outstanding sportsmen and had scored the winning goal for his team in the finals game. He was in his mid-thirties and an extremely fit person physically.

The operation to recover the vehicle and the soldiers from the accident site was becoming tougher in the dark and under incessant firing from the other side of the border. After persistent efforts, the recovery party accomplished the task of moving the body of the driver and the co-driver who, fortunately, had not been injured, to a safe area. The tasks for me now involved the coordination of efforts to shift the body of the killed soldier to the base location. Recovery operations were continued to retrieve the damaged vehicle.

At around 1:30 A.M., I received another call from the MI room informing me that the condition of the person who had been brought in earlier has started deteriorating. I called for the junior officer who was at the base and requested he goes to the medical room and check out the situation there. The officer reached the medical rooms in about fifteen minutes and called me to say that the patient's condition appeared to be critical. After a quick chat with the medical assistant, we decided to move the patient immediately to the field hospital located about five kilometres away. In operational areas near the LoC, the movement of vehicles at night is banned. For emergencies, it was required to get permission from the higher HQ. However, considering the situation that we were in the urgency for better medical care for the patient, I asked the medical room in charge to move out with the vehicle immediately. I got back to coordinating the operations on the LoC which continued till the next day's break.

The following morning, the CO returned to the base and he was called to the brigade HQ for immediate debriefing. The stranded vehicle was still stuck at the accident site, and the next phase of the operations to recover it had to be planned.

At around 7 A.M., I went to the adjutant's office to check the standard operating procedures (SOPs) for handling casualties. As I was reading through them, I received an urgent call from the brigade HQ, our CO was online and he asked me, "C. T., did you move someone to the field hospital last night?" I answered in affirmative and quickly narrated the background. After hearing me and a brief pause, the CO said, "You know what...he is no more." This sounded like a bomb explosion and I sank into my chair dumbfounded. The CO understood my silence and said, "Don't worry. It is just one of those days when things go bad. I will come back in a while, and we can discuss the next steps."

While his words were indeed a great relief, I was weighed down by various thoughts. Did I make a mistake by not addressing the medical issue in the right manner when it was reported to me last night? There are two death cases in the Unit now and what would be the impact of these two deaths in quick succession on the morale of the troops? How should I manage the questions from the HQ? I had gotten into the operation on the LoC at 6 PM the previous evening which continued the whole night through the morning, not having eaten anything and not even getting the time to take off my shoes. I was completely exhausted already and this new turn of events drained me out completely and froze me to the chair.

At this point, the second-in-command (2IC) walked into my office. He was an experienced person' however even he was baffled by this situation in front of us. We discussed the deeply disturbing situation. After pondering for some time, he said let us ask for a cup of strong tea. This helped us to shake off the shock lethargy and we started putting together the action steps that needed to be followed. The 2IC took on the task of handling the medical case and asked me to continue to concentrate on operations in progress on the LoC to recover the stranded vehicle.

The rest of the day was hectic- the weapons firing from the other side of the LoC became more intense and accurate in the daylight. However, as we could put the required mechanization to pull up the vehicle, it could be finally retrieved at around 2 P.M.

The 2IC and I walked around the base camp, meeting and talking to the troops to assuage their concern and bolster their morale. The last rites of the two soldiers were conducted at the base location as per military tradition by about 4 PM. It was indeed one of the longest, saddest, and most challenging days in my professional career. The follow-up actions including various fact-finding inquiries, and other procedures, were completed in the days ahead, as per army rules and procedure.

In one of the earlier case references in this book about the incident in Sri Lanka, I mentioned the learning the need to be prepared for the unexpected – especially while deployed in an operational area. However, a crisis tends to surprise with double whammies such as narrated in this case. As the severity of this incident had attracted the attention of senior command echelons, the onus of ensuring a prompt and accurate flow of information to them while being busy coordinating the operational support on the ground was an enormous responsibility.

Key learnings on crisis leadership, crisis handling and resilience from this incident are as follows:

1. **Concurrent Crisis Help Build Personal Resilience:** The ability to cope with and withstand stress gets accentuated and enhanced as we deal with multiple concurrent perils. As a leader, one would have no choice but to deal with such requirements stoically. Mental agility and endurance help to be more resilient to face challenging situations.

2. **Prioritization and focus are essential when dealing with multiple crises:** In a multi-crisis scenario, the leader would be required to devote focus as required for each incident or situation, even when they are not directly correlated. The leader needs to keep the mind space to absorb such unexpected developments; however, it is important to assign priorities and mobilize available support and resources to address the specific requirements of a variety of situational demands.

3. **Critical Thinking and speed of decision are critical in a concurrent crisis:** In an evolving situation, the timing of decisions is key. One may not get the opportunity to evaluate options and would need to act with limited resources and respond. The leader would need to be quick to critically analyze the incidents and decide on actions. The decision to task the young officer to check on the medical case and move the patient in a vehicle to the hospital at night were quick decisions in the thick of actions.

4. **Empathy, trust, and reassurance ensure positivity and motivation:** In a crisis where the situation is changing rapidly and multiple challenges are to be dealt with concurrently, it is likely that some of the decisions and actions could be hasty and will not result in the desired outcomes. The crisis leader needs to show empathy and help build a sense of trust and reassurance. In this narration, the CO's immediate reaction to the medical case situation and the second-in-command stepping up to support when the morale was at the lowest, are examples of a combination of these attributes.

5. **Maintaining a state of high Morale in a crisis is essential:** The morale of people plays a vital role in facing up to a crisis and it boots the development of personal resilience. When a concurrent crisis occurs in quick succession, the morale takes a beating and subsides quickly. The leader holds the added responsibility to prevent this from occurring. It is important to remain calm, composed and reassuring to keep the confidence and spirit of the team. The response by the CO when he spoke to me about the

second casualty and the reassuring action by the 2IC walking up to me when I was in a state of complete shock and helping me get out of that mindset are examples of this. As the morale of the entire team of troops in the base location was impacted by these two sad incidents, it was important to boost positivity, which was achieved as the 2IC went around the camp talking with the troops present there.

RESILIENCE SUMMARY

Every crisis puts intense stress and strain on people and processes at the individual and organizational levels. On many such occasions, the odds may seem insurmountable, however, a properly orchestrated response mechanism bolstered with the experience and learning of living through such situations in the past strengthens the resolve. This contributes towards individuals and organizations becoming more resilient with each passing crisis.

The life lessons one gathers from these experiences will differ from person to person, as it depends on multiple factors such as the situation, the role one plays in a crisis, actions, and reactions concerning the situation and the outcome. These experiences will also be unique for a person designated to lead in a crisis (the leader), others who work through the situation in diverse roles (the team - the led), and those impacted by the situation.

Resilience, at the individual level, is the most critical trait that triggers a positive response in a crisis. This is also a characteristic acquired, forged, and reinforced by adversities and consequential triumphs and tribulations. Individual resilience is deeply rooted in psychological resilience and this is multifaceted. There is much research on the subject and academically many theories are available on the tools and techniques to develop this which is not in the scope of this book. The focus of this book is limited to highlighting the most obvious characteristics that contribute to resilience as demonstrated by leaders and teams in practical crisis scenarios at the operational level. From the experiences as narrated the key characteristics that help build resilience at the individual level are, being adaptive, flexible, agile and emotionally strong.

Organizational resilience is the ability to resist the impact of any disruption and be able to rebound and continue to progress even after a disruption. There is a lot of study and research in this area as well. However, from practical experience it is learnt that to be resilient organizations need to have proper structures to delineate ownership and accountability, provides a safe and secure work environment focusing on the week being of people, the workforce is empowered and there is a culture of continuous learning which leverages on the experience from the lived crisis experiences. To bring all these into effect the most important is the involvement and commitment of the leadership.

In essence, every crisis acts as a crucible that forges resilience at the individual, leadership and organizational levels.

CASE REFERENCES – RESILIENCE IN CRISIS

SPACE FOR READER'S REFLECTIONS

....
....
....
....
....
....
....
....
....
....
....
....
....
....
....
....
....
....
....
....

9

Crisis and Business Continuity Management in the Emerging World

Any crisis is bound to have an impact on the organization in various ways such as operational, financial, environmental, legal and regulatory related, health and safety of people and most importantly reputational. The severity of impact depends on the nature of the crisis and its effect on people and processes. In an isolated crisis scenario such as a one off natural calamity, failure of critical infrastructure or a man-made disaster may only have a limited impact on the organization as it can be managed with quick response actions. However, a major crisis having multi locational impact such as the global pandemic will certainly cripple operations and business at a much larger scale and therefore the impact would be more debilitating and risking the continuity of business and organization.

Crisis management and business continuity management are not mutually exclusive. A robust business continuity plan need to anticipate potential crisis scenarios that could impact the business with clearly defined response mechanism to avoid or reduce the impact. Business continuity management is a subset of the overall enterprise level risk management and therefore crisis management also assumes significant importance from an enterprise risk management perspective.

Traditionally, organizations were focusing on localized crisis scenarios and response plans. However, covid pandemic and the resultant impact on the global supply chains has exposed the inadequacy of this fractured approach of business continuity management. With the hyper connected global business ecosystem and the increased probability of disruptions attributable to various causes such as climate change, geo-political issues, wars and conflicts renders businesses significantly vulnerable. In this emerging scenario, business organizations need to be prepared to deal with disruptive events of much larger scale and significant debilitating impact on business continuity.

The role of business and risk management leaders has become more complex in this emerging scenario. They are expected to visualize potential scenarios that can have a disruptive impact on the business including the upstream and downstream value chains and implement mitigation plans. This calls for continuous scanning of global risk scenarios and readjustment of the enterprise risk and business continuity management framework. The plans would need to constantly evolve to address all such scenarios with appropriate response. This development signifies that business continuity management cannot be a support function – rather it would need to be in the strategic core of the business plans not only within the organization but including the supply chain and partner ecosystems-especially the last mile.

In the emerging global risk scenarios, the traditional business continuity and crisis response models would be found inadequate. The organizational capability on business continuity management needs to be predictive both at the strategic and operational levels, so as to pre-empt any disruption to business rather than respond in a reactive manner after the occurrence of a disruptive event. There are various agencies and subject matter experts who continuously monitor the various aspects such as economy, climate, geo-politics and security conflicts to cite a few examples, at the country and global levels. Based on these indicators these agencies put together reports on emerging risks. These reports help organizations to compile the strategic enterprise risk registers and the planned mitigation for the identified risks.

At the operational level, technology can play a vital role to predict potential disruptive scenarios. As an example applications based on IoT (Internet of Things) and artificial intelligence can provide predictive analytics to forecast potential failure of critical equipment. Similarly solutions based on advanced robotics can deployed to reduce risk to human lives where physical intervention to manage a crisis is unavoidable. A highly intelligent technology platform with the capabilities to predict potential adverse scenarios that can impact the business negatively and simulate the probable response to such scenarios, will aid overall business continuity management.

The hyper connected environment also calls for collaborative approach where all parties in the business ecosystem come together rather than limit the business continuity plans to isolated business environments. Continuity of a business is not guaranteed if that is not assured outside the organization with a critical player in the value chain. An integrated model for business continuity would be an essential requirement in the days ahead. This would necessitate a higher degree of collaboration among the entire business eco system.

The future scenarios for crisis and business continuity will be complex. While there would be increased dependence on collaboration and innovative technology solutions to manage business continuity, the element of human intervention will continue to be critical. The role of business risk and business continuity professionals will be critical firstly, to identify and deploy the appropriate methods and tools and then to orchestrate the interplay of people and technology to derive the desired outcomes. Being adept with technology will be a critical skill requirement for risk professionals.

The important question is can technology alone manage all crises and ensure business continuity wholistically? The answer is an emphatic "no." Even with the most advanced technology solutions, crisis management would remain a process that is driven and enabled by people. Therefore the interplay of crisis leadership, team dynamics and resilience would continue to be paramount, which can be enhanced and accelerated with technology.

Being challenged in life is inevitable ... being defeated is optional.

Acknowledgements

This compilation is a result of the consistent nudging and encouragement from my colleagues, past and present, which is truly appreciated.

I am immensely thankful to Dr EJ Sarma and Col SM Kumar for the foreword and introductions and Supriya Singh for the first reader comments.

Appreciations to my colleagues Pallavi Barua, and Shalini Sasi and my daughters, Neelima & Namitha and my niece Anu, for their comprehensive value-additions to the script at various stages.

Profound appreciation to my past colleague Sanjiv Tare for his valuable input on the contents.

Thanks to Rajan Arya and the editorial team of Pentagon Press LLP.

And finally, a heap of thanks to my wife, Meenakshi, for being a pillar of strength through these years and for her seamless support while penning this script.

Glossary of Terms

Adjutant	Staff officer to the Commanding Officer in an Army unit
BCP	Business Continuity Plan
BCM	Business Continuity Management
BIA	Business Impact Analysis
BM	Brigade Major; a role like the adjutant at the formation level
CAB	COVID-Appropriate Behaviour
CO	Commanding Officer, the Leader responsible for running the unit
CST	Chhatrapati Shivaji Terminus – the main railway station in Mumbai, India
Field Hospital	Second-level and better equipped medical facility in an operational area
HQ	Headquarters
LoC	Line of Control; the boundary line between two countries without the demarcation of a no-man's-land in

	between, as would be in the case of international borders
MI Room	Medical Inspection Room in a unit where first-level treatment is given
Officer Commanding	The leader responsible for running a subunit in an infantry unit
Officers' Mess	The facility in an army unit where the commissioned officers dine
PRO	Public Relations Officer
QRT	Quick Reaction Team
ROP	Road Opening Patrol
Subunit	Operational organization a level below the unit; normally, a company of troops
2IC Second in Command	the number 2 person after the commanding office in an army unit
Unit	An operational level organization in the army; normally a battalion of troops
VUCA	a Term indicating "Volatile, Uncertain, Complex, Ambiguous" general conditions and situations.

DISCLAIMER

The case references in this book are real life incidents. Due care has been taken to ensure privacy; however any inconsistency is purely unintentional.

The author has referred to various open source articles available on the internet for theoretical explanation of the terms leadership, team dynamics and resilience.

Index